Tastes, Tales and Traditions

Tastes, Tales and Traditions

Published by the Palo Alto Auxiliary for Children
Copyright © 2005 by the Palo Alto
    Auxiliary for Children
75 Arbor Road, Suite C
Menlo Park, California 94025
650-324-2588

This cookbook is a collection of our favorite
recipes, not necessarily original recipes.

Library of Congress Control Number:
    20059424988

ISBN: 0-9766338-0-9

Edited, Designed, and Manufactured by
Favorite Recipes® Press
an imprint of

FRP

P.O. Box 305142
Nashville, Tennessee 37230
800-358-0560

Art Direction and book design: Steve Newman
Editorial Director: Mary Cummings
Project Editor: Tanis Westbrook

Manufactured in China
First Printing 2005
5,000 copies

Art Acknowledgments

Paintings are from original watercolors and oils
© Auxiliary member and professional artist
Carolyn Hofstetter.

Photographs © Auxiliary members Shirlee Stites,
Betty Plemons, and Eleanor Settle.

Illustrations by Auxiliary member Stephanie
Wood-Smith and freelance illustrator Barbara Ball.

On the cover: Garden of Abundance at Allied Arts Guild
in Menlo Park, California, by Carolyn Hofstetter.

Tastes, Tales and Traditions

Presented by the Palo Alto Auxiliary For Children

Benefiting Lucile Salter Packard Children's Hospital

Dedication

Over the years, local and neighboring communities have
come to view Allied Arts Guild Restaurant as a symbol.
That symbol represents the hearts and minds of Palo Alto Auxiliary volunteers
who give their time and energy so that children suffering from serious illness
might receive the finest medical attention.
It also represents the careful planning and diverse skills that are vital to keeping the
Restaurant prosperous while, at the same time, serving its customers in a most enjoyable way.

To all volunteers of the Palo Alto Auxiliary
Who never lose sight of their mission,
Who continuously strive for higher goals,
Who personify the symbol of Allied Arts Guild Restaurant,

To all these volunteers
Past, present, and future
This book is lovingly dedicated.

Foreword

    The Palo Alto Auxiliary has a successful seventy-year history distinguished by its two very important missions—to operate the wonderful, all-volunteer Allied Arts Guild Restaurant and to provide generous financial support for uncompensated medical care given to children in need at Lucile Salter Packard Children's Hospital.

    With this cookbook, the Auxiliary combines these missions into a splendid publication that will help support the Hospital as it brings us years of enjoyment.

    I am honored to have the outstanding commitment of Palo Alto Auxiliary members and their many friends and supporters in the community. You help the Hospital and the children and families we serve with every visit to the Allied Arts Guild Restaurant, and now, with every purchase of this cookbook that will be treasured in your homes and by your families.

With deepest thanks,

Harvey J. Cohen

Harvey J. Cohen, M.D., Ph.D.
Chief of Staff, Lucile Salter Packard Children's Hospital
Chairman, Department of Pediatrics
Stanford University School of Medicine

Preface

The Palo Alto Auxiliary for Children, Inc.
A member of The Association of Auxiliaries Corporation for Children

In the beginning ...

In 1931, the Palo Alto Auxiliary was established to raise funds for convalescing children. Members created and sold Christmas wreaths made out of lacquered laurel leaves and small crab apples. They also sold surplus fruit and flowers from their own gardens on a street corner, as well as pencils at the neighborhood train station. For extra funds, they employed their culinary skills by hosting teas, as they continued to search for ways to raise more funds for their cause.

A unique and creative place ...

In 1929, a crafts guild of Spanish colonial design, constructed on three and one-half acres of land in Menlo Park, California, was born. Resonating all the charm of the craft guilds in Europe, this distinctive place of beauty was named Allied Arts Guild. Conceived as a place of tranquility, artists gathered to create handmade objects of special quality, including wrought iron, woodwork, pottery, hand block textiles, handwoven fabrics, photo engraving, hand-tooled leather, and sculpture.

A role in culinary arts ...

In 1932, the owners of Allied Arts Guild offered the Palo Alto Auxiliary a role in culinary arts by asking the members to provide luncheon service at the Guild. What an opportunity for these ladies—a chance to increase their charitable donations by serving the community in a most creative way. Members were trained to be proficient in the skills of correct table setting and gracious service. Meals were served in one of three places: 1) the serenity of the Guild's main building, 2) the inner court known as Cervantes, or 3) the Garden of Delight, showcasing the wisteria-covered terrace by the lilacs. Luncheon was by reservation only. Since a restaurant had not been included in the plans for the Guild complex, there was no kitchen. Auxiliary members prepared the meals in their own homes and brought them to the Guild to serve. The kitchen facilities consisted of a coffeemaker and a two-burner hot plate. On the first day of business eight guests were served, and the Auxiliary earned $6.00. In the first years, luncheon was served six days a week. Service for twenty guests was considered a big day.

A *reorganization & expansion*...

Due to the early success of the Restaurant, the Auxiliary's membership increased significantly. A proper kitchen was added to the complex, and a business manager as well as kitchen assistants were hired. This reorganization also allowed the Auxiliary to host fashion shows, teas, bridal showers, wedding receptions, and private parties. By 2000, the yearly events that continued to thrive and sell out included the Valentine's Day Tea, Bunny Days, Mother's Day Luncheon and Fashion Show, An American Girl Doll Event, and the Holiday Tea. In addition, the Auxiliary continued to host wedding receptions and bridal showers, as well as offer the terrace to social bridge players, followed by lunch. Membership expanded to over 200 active members who worked in the Restaurant each month, as well as over 200 associate members. In 2001, the Restaurant hosted 27,000 guests.

A *mission accomplished*...

By 1950, the Auxiliary was able to underwrite the cost of five children and to establish a $20,000 Endowment Fund with a second endowment completed by the mid-1950s. Since that time, contributions have increased significantly due to the creativity, imagination, and dedication of the members devoted to their mission:

> *To promote, foster, and maintain the welfare of children and*
> *to raise funds for the Lucile Packard Children's Hospital at Stanford.*

Funds raised by the Palo Alto Auxiliary continue to pay for the care of seriously ill children who would otherwise be unable to afford the medical help they desperately need.

A *reopening celebration*...

In 2002, the Allied Arts Guild closed to renovate the one-hundred-year-old infrastructure on the complex. However, some things will never change. The Palo Alto Auxiliary and the Allied Arts Guild have been inseparable for more than seventy years. The volunteers will be back at work, full speed ahead in celebration of the reopening. The Restaurant will flourish and stay alive with fresh new volunteers. Like volunteers of the past, the new members will continue to operate, staff, and maintain the Restaurant for charitable purposes. They will continue to bring new and innovative ideas to the luncheon service and, like volunteers of the past, will never lose sight of their mission.

This book commemorates the first seventy years of Allied Arts Restaurant,

A legacy to remember . . .
And celebrates the reopening,
A new beginning . . .

Introduction

Tastes, Tales and Traditions is more than just a cookbook. It is a legacy to the hundreds of dedicated and hardworking members of the Palo Alto Auxiliary. These volunteers, in support of the Lucile Packard Children's Hospital at Stanford, have unceasingly given of their time and energy to promote the success and profitability of the Allied Arts Guild Restaurant. This, too, is their story. In this book, we invite you to stroll down the paths of the beautiful gardens, enjoy the historic Spanish art, and marvel at the century-old architectural features. Then, step through the front door of the Restaurant, and behold its charming ambience. Seventy years of *Tastes, Tales and Traditions* await you here.

The *Tastes* include recipes culled from the Restaurant's voluminous and varied collection, supplemented by favorites from current members. Each and every recipe in this book has survived rigorous testing and evaluating by our own skilled volunteers. Only the very best have been selected for this book. We have included many recipes that span the decades and have remained popular with our customers despite ever-changing food tastes. Whether you are looking for a recipe for an ethnic-inspired dish, a recipe that will take you back to the remembered comfort and informality of your mother's kitchen, or a recipe for an elegant dish to serve at your next dinner party, you are sure to find one that will please.

The *Tales*, scattered throughout the sidebars, consist of the informational vignettes and fun-filled anecdotes from the rich history of this organization. In a most enjoyable manner, these tales will help you visualize the style and mood of the Restaurant, as well as the camaraderie of its members and the strength of their mission.

Entrance to the Restaurant

The *Traditions*, featured in the chapter headings, describe the yearly, sellout events followed by sample menus. These traditions include our Valentine's Day Tea, Bunny Days, Mother's Day Luncheon and Fashion Show, Weddings and Receptions, Monday Morning Bridge, An American Girl Event, Holiday Tea, and Holiday Luncheons. Please read on to discover for yourself why these events have blossomed into such beloved traditions and why Allied Arts Guild Restaurant has continued to flourish for so many years.

Enjoy!

Contents

Front Gate

Teatime Favorites

Valentine's Day Tea

It is not surprising that the Valentine's Day Tea is one of the most popular events at Allied Arts Guild Restaurant. After all, the Palo Alto Auxiliary has been organizing successful teas for decades. Now and then, friends and couples should take a little "time-out" to say how much they appreciate each other. The Valentine's Day Tea is the perfect opportunity.

What makes this mid-February event an annual sellout is its extraordinary attention to detail. Volunteers work for weeks planning and implementing a menu that includes items sweet and savory, hot and cold, crispy and smooth, dense and lighter-than-air.

On the day of the tea, cooks place items in precise locations on the tea plates—always an odd number on each plate—and garnish each plate with a dewy-fresh California camellia before it enters the dining room. Servers circulate around the dining room with sterling silver teapots and coffeepots brought from home—graciously dispensing hot beverages to the guests. Iced black currant tea is also available for those who desire it. With at least nine items on the tea plate and all the tea you can drink, it is generally agreed that the portions are more than generous.

Live harp music fills the air as the guests settle in for a "wee bit" more tea. There is no show, no program, no agenda to interrupt the gentle flow of conversation from the tables. Even though another seating will follow, there is no feeling of rush.

Gone are the days when all the guests wore hats and gloves. However, the more important traditions of fine food and gracious service remain and have only grown stronger over the years. Modern menus, lovely music, a beautiful view, and sterling silver service have made today's Valentine's Day Tea truly the *Jewel in the Crown*.

Allied Arts Guild Restaurant Presents

Valentine's Day Tea

February 14

Menu

Smoked Salmon Tea Sandwiches
On Dark Rye with Caper Dill Relish
Parmesan Twists
Almond Ham Triangles on Cracked Wheat
Watercress Tomato Roulade
Dilled Egg Triangles
Asparagus Roll-Ups
Hot Artichoke Parmesan Squares
Polka Dot Cookies
Mini-Lemon Cheesecake Bites with Cherry Topping
Chocolate Mint Bars
Hot Earl Grey Tea
Iced Black Currant Tea
Coffee

Live Harp Music

Benefiting Lucile Packard Children's Hospital at Stanford

Orange and Cinnamon Breadsticks

Yield: about 60 orange and 60 cinnamon breadsticks

Two of the Restaurant's old teatime favorites, always baked at the same time and served together, have been kept a closely guarded secret . . . until now! The recipe requires two days in the making.

Orange Jubilee Topping

Yield: 5 cups

4 oranges, washed, cut into chunks and seeded
2 lemons, washed, cut into chunks and seeded
1¹/4 cups sugar
1 (8-ounce) can crushed pineapple, drained

Cinnamon Topping

Yield: 1 cup

2 teaspoons cinnamon
1 cup sugar

Breadsticks

1 Pullman loaf or 1 loaf French toast bread, crusts trimmed
   and cut into 1-inch slices
¹/2 cup (1 stick) butter, melted

For the orange topping, coarsely grind the oranges and lemons, including the skins, in a food processor fitted with a steel blade. Combine the ground fruit, sugar and pineapple in a bowl, stirring until the sugar is dissolved. Chill for 1 day to 2 weeks or freeze.

For the cinnamon topping, combine the cinnamon and sugar in a small shallow bowl.

For the breadsticks, line a large baking sheet with foil and grease the foil. Preheat the broiler. Cut the bread slices into 1×2-inch sticks, about 4 per slice. Brush the top and bottom of each stick with the butter and place on the prepared baking sheet. Broil until the tops are golden brown. Cool and store, tightly sealed, for 1 day. Line a large baking sheet with foil and grease the foil. Spread 1¹/2 teaspoons Orange Jubilee Topping on the untoasted side of ¹/2 of the breadsticks. Roll the remaining breadsticks in the Cinnamon Topping. Place the breadsticks on the prepared baking sheet. Broil until hot and bubbly. Serve hot. Make Orange Jubilee Spread (see sidebar) with any leftover topping.

Something Old, Something New

When we found the recipe for Orange and Cinnamon Breadsticks in our massive collection, we were reminded of the days our grandmothers cooked with a pinch of this and a handful of that. For example, the instructions were handwritten and full of descriptive words from that generation:

"Butter and 'stick' under broiler until you think they're done. Put orange 'goop' just on the top side. Broil just until sticks have gotten a little crisp on sides—not soggy."

Also, none of the ingredients called for exact measurements:

"Mix cinnamon and sugar together—no particular measurements—just what you think you'll need."

Even though the original recipe was so open to interpretation, to our amazement, the volunteers produced perfect breadsticks for every Tea. We hope today's busy cooks will find this version more foolproof.

Orange Jubilee Spread

8 ounces cream cheese
¹/3 cup Orange Jubilee Topping
¹/3 teaspoon ground ginger

Beat cream cheese until smooth. Add Orange Jubilee Topping and ginger. Beat until thoroughly incorporated. Spread on toast, pound cake, or biscuits.

Strawberry Bread

Yield: 2 loaves

Cinnamon enhances the fruity flavor of this moist bread. Serve as is or with Strawberry Butter.

  3 cups all-purpose flour
  2 cups sugar
  1 tablespoon cinnamon
  1 teaspoon baking soda
  1 teaspoon salt
  $1^1/4$ cups chopped walnuts, toasted
  1 (16-ounce) package frozen unsweetened strawberries, thawed and
    drained for 30 minutes
  4 eggs, beaten
  $1^1/4$ cups vegetable oil
  Strawberry Butter (optional)

Grease two 5×9-inch loaf pans. Line the pans with parchment paper or waxed paper, if desired. Preheat the oven to 350 degrees. Combine the flour, sugar, cinnamon, baking soda, salt and walnuts in a large bowl. Chop the strawberries in a food processor by pulsing 3 times. Add the strawberries, eggs and oil to the flour mixture, stirring just until mixed. Pour into the prepared pans. Bake for 1 hour or until the loaves test done. Cool in the pans on a wire rack for 5 minutes. Remove from the pans and cool completely before slicing. Serve with Strawberry Butter.

Strawberry Butter

Yield: $^3/4$ cup

This spread is wonderful served with our Strawberry Bread, Best-Ever Bran Muffins (page 44), and just about any other sweet quick bread, biscuits, muffins, toast, pancakes, or waffles.

  $^1/2$ cup (1 stick) unsalted butter, softened
  3 tablespoons strawberry preserves (use a premium grade)
  $^1/8$ teaspoon rum extract
  2 tablespoons confectioners' sugar, or to taste

Combine the butter, strawberry preserves and rum extract in a bowl and mix well. Stir in the confectioners' sugar.

Lemon Tea Bread

Yield: 1 loaf

Awaken your taste buds at breakfast, brunch, or lunch with the tangy zest of fresh lemons in this quick loaf—a tea menu favorite at the Restaurant. Serve it with Orange Jubilee Spread (page 16), if desired.

> 1/2 cup (1 stick) butter, softened
> 1 cup sugar
> 2 eggs, lightly beaten
> 1 teaspoon vanilla extract
> Grated zest of 2 lemons
> 1 1/4 cups all-purpose flour
> 1 teaspoon baking powder
> 1 teaspoon salt
> 1/2 cup milk
> 1/2 cup finely chopped walnuts

Grease a 5×9-inch loaf pan. Line the pan with parchment paper or waxed paper, if desired. Preheat the oven to 350 degrees. Cream the butter and sugar in a mixing bowl until light and fluffy. Beat in the eggs, vanilla and lemon zest. Combine the flour, baking powder and salt in a small bowl. Stir 1/2 of the flour mixture into the creamed mixture. Stir in 1/2 of the milk. Repeat with the remaining flour mixture and milk, stirring just until mixed. Stir in the walnuts. Pour into the prepared pan. Bake for 45 to 60 minutes or until the loaf tests done. Cool in the pan on a wire rack for 5 minutes. Remove from the pan and cool completely before slicing.

Early Days of Tea Service

In 1951 the Palo Alto Auxiliary took charge of the daily afternoon tea service at Allied Arts Guild. Tea was served on tea tables created by the talented original artisan of the woodshop. The tables were light green and were crafted with handles so they could be carried to wherever the guests wished to sit. Two ladies might sit by the fireplace or on a bench in the Blue Garden by the wild lilacs. Servers would bring the tea tables to them. Later, as the number of customers grew from ten to more than one hundred per day, guests were seated at the luncheon tables.

The very first placemats were straw. These were replaced with chartreuse mats from the weaving studio at the Guild, which complemented the floral design on the pottery dishes.

Tea foods were originally presented on large plates served at each table and passed around "family style" to each guest. This proved unsatisfactory because lots of food was wasted. No one wanted to appear rude by taking the last piece on the plate! To remedy this, food service was changed to provide individual tea plates for each guest. From then on, empty plates came back to the kitchen with no waste.

Stuffed Baguettes

Yield: about 20 slices per baguette

Baguettes of French bread are hollowed, stuffed with your choice of filling, and sliced to make these favorite teatime sandwiches. They may be prepared the day before serving. Each filling option makes about 1 1/2 cups.

> 1 baguette of French bread (regular or
>   sourdough)
> 1 1/2 cups of 1 of the fillings listed below
> Milk

Trim the ends from the baguette and cut in half lengthwise. Hollow out the center of each bread half, leaving a little bread under the crust on all sides. Thin the filling with milk if necessary to reach a piping consistency. Spoon the filling into a pastry tube fitted with a large open tip. Pipe into the hollow of each bread half. Reassemble the two halves. Chill, tightly wrapped, in plastic wrap, for 8 hours. To serve, slice the baguette into 1/2- to 3/4-inch pieces. Arrange the slices on a platter and cover with plastic wrap until serving time. Serve at room temperature.

Sun-Dried Tomato Filling

> 3/4 cup (3 ounces) shredded Cheddar cheese
> 4 ounces cream cheese, softened
> 3/4 cup finely chopped sun-dried tomatoes
>   (not marinated)
> 2 teaspoons Italian herbs
> 1/4 teaspoon dry mustard

Combine the Cheddar cheese, cream cheese, sun-dried tomatoes, Italian herbs and dry mustard in a small bowl and mix well.

Artichoke Parmesan Filling

> 1 cup Artichoke Parmesan Topping (page 24)
> 1/4 cup chopped canned water-packed
>   artichoke bottoms
> 4 ounces cream cheese, softened
> 1/8 teaspoon cayenne pepper

Combine the Artichoke Parmesan Topping, artichokes, cream cheese and pepper in a small bowl and mix well.

Mushroom Pâté Filling

> 1 cup Exotic Mushroom Pâté, softened
>   (page 46)
> 4 ounces cream cheese, softened

Combine the Exotic Mushroom Pâté and cream cheese in a small bowl and mix well.

Spinach Filling

> 1/3 of 1 (10-ounce) package frozen chopped
>   spinach, thawed, squeezed dry and
>   chopped again
> 1/2 of 1 envelope leek soup mix
> 1/2 cup sour cream
> 4 ounces cream cheese, softened

Combine the spinach, soup mix, sour cream and cream cheese in a small bowl and mix well.

Liverwurst Pâté Filling

> 1 cup Liverwurst Pâté Spread (page 47)
> 3 ounces cream cheese, softened
> 1 garlic clove, minced
> 1 tablespoon chopped green onions

Combine the Liverwurst Pâté Spread, cream cheese, garlic and green onions in a small bowl and mix well.

Ribbon Tea Sandwiches

Yield: 6 whole sandwiches or 24 tea sandwiches

Layers of cream cheese and olives give these finger sandwiches an appeal that no one can resist. Chill them for at least two hours before slicing and serving.

12 ounces cream cheese, softened
1/2 cup finely chopped celery
1/2 cup finely chopped toasted slivered almonds
2 teaspoons milk
Pepper to taste
12 slices thin wheat bread
12 slices thin white bread
1 (7-ounce) jar pimento-stuffed green olives, drained and thinly sliced

Combine the cream cheese, celery, almonds, milk and pepper in a bowl and mix well. Spread each of the wheat and white bread slices with 1 tablespoon of the cream cheese mixture. Top 1 white bread slice with 1 wheat slice, cream cheese mixture facing up. Spread 1/6 of the sliced olives over the wheat slice. Top with another white slice, cream cheese mixture facing down. Top with another wheat slice, cream cheese mixture facing down. Repeat the procedure to make the remaining 5 sandwiches. Place sandwiches on a tray and cover with a damp towel. Cover tightly with plastic wrap. Chill for 2 to 8 hours. Trim the crusts and cut each sandwich into 4 fingers for tea-size portions. Refrigerate, tightly wrapped, until serving time.

The "Tea Bags"

For many years the organization for tea service at Allied Arts Guild Restaurant included a separate group of veteran volunteers. The younger volunteers were unable to work late in the afternoon because they had the responsibility of children coming home from school.

Consequently, the tea volunteer organization consisted of women who did not have younger children. Tea service was a good fit for these women, who were usually older and well trained in all aspects of preparing and serving teas. These ladies began to refer to themselves affectionately as the "Tea Bags."

San Francisco columnist Herb Caen heard "through the grapevine" that these ladies called themselves the "Tea Bags," and he wrote quite an amusing article about them in his famous column in the San Francisco Chronicle. This article increased the popularity of the "Tea Bags" throughout the community. Everyone loved the "Tea Bags."

Curried Shrimp and Cucumber Tea Sandwiches

Yield: about 40 tea sandwiches

Almost too attractive to eat, these canapés will generate "oohs and aahs" from your guests.

> 1 English cucumber
> Salt
> 1 pound peeled cooked bay shrimp,
>   finely chopped
> 3 tablespoons minced onion
> 1¹/₂ tablespoons mayonnaise, or enough
>   to blend
> 1 tablespoon lemon juice
> ¹/₂ teaspoon Worcestershire sauce
> 2 dashes of Tabasco sauce
> ¹/₂ teaspoon curry powder
> Salt and pepper to taste
> White or wheat bread

Peel thin vertical strips of skin from the cucumber, leaving a pattern of alternating green and white strips. Cut the cucumber into ¹/₈-inch slices. Place the cucumbers in a colander and sprinkle generously with salt. Let stand for 30 minutes. Rinse the cucumbers; drain and pat dry with paper towels. Combine the shrimp, onion, mayonnaise, lemon juice, Worcestershire sauce, Tabasco sauce, curry powder, salt and pepper in a bowl and mix well. Cut the bread into rounds the same size as the cucumber slices. Place a cucumber slice on top of each bread round. Top with a scant teaspoon of the shrimp mixture. Garnish with finely chopped Italian parsley, small sprigs of dill weed or additional bay shrimp.

Smoked Salmon Tea Sandwiches

Yield: 24 tea sandwiches

What makes these canapés so irresistible is the dollop of Caper-Dill Relish that adorns the top of each one.

> 6 ounces cream cheese, softened
> 1 tablespoon (or more) milk
> 24 thin slices sourdough baguette, cocktail
>   rye or pumpernickel bread
> 6 ounces lox-style smoked salmon, thinly
>   sliced and cut into 24 pieces
> Caper-Dill Relish

Beat the cream cheese and milk together in a small bowl. Add enough milk to reach spreading consistency. Spread ¹/₂ tablespoon of the cream cheese mixture on each bread slice. Top each slice with a piece of salmon and about ³/₄ teaspoon Caper-Dill Relish. Garnish with a small sprig of dill weed.

Caper-Dill Relish

> ¹/₄ cup finely chopped white onion
> 1 tablespoon drained capers
> 2 tablespoons chopped fresh dill weed,
>   tightly packed
> 1 tablespoon plus 1 teaspoon Dijon mustard
> 1 tablespoon fresh lemon juice
> Salt and pepper to taste

Combine the onion, capers, dill weed, Dijon mustard and lemon juice in a small bowl and mix well. Stir in the salt and pepper. Let stand to blend flavors.

Walnut Chili Chicken Filling

Yield: 1 3/4 cups

Do something special with your leftover chicken by making this savory crunchy spread.

> 1 cup finely chopped cooked chicken
> 1/2 cup finely chopped walnuts, toasted
> 3 tablespoons canned diced green chiles
> 2 tablespoons finely chopped green onions
> 1 tablespoon finely chopped cilantro
> 1/2 teaspoon chili powder
> 1/4 teaspoon salt
> 1/8 teaspoon pepper
> 1/2 cup mayonnaise

Combine the chicken, walnuts, chiles, green onions, cilantro, chili powder, salt, pepper and mayonnaise in a bowl and mix well. Adjust the seasonings to taste.

Dilled Egg Filling

Yield: 1 1/2 cups

This subtle blend of flavors will add new life to that next tea sandwich.

> 6 hard-cooked eggs, peeled and chopped
> 2 green onions, minced
> 2 tablespoons dill relish
> 1/4 teaspoon dry mustard
> 1/4 to 1/2 cup mayonnaise
> Salt and pepper to taste

Mash the eggs to a fine consistency in a small bowl. Stir in the green onions, relish, dry mustard and enough mayonnaise to reach a spreading consistency. Add the salt and pepper. Chill, covered, for 8 hours.

Tea Sandwich Process

Assemble: Spread one-fourth to one-third cup filling between two slices of bread. If not serving right away, place sandwiches on a baking sheet. Top with a slightly damp towel. Cover tightly with plastic wrap and refrigerate for up to eight hours.

Trim crusts from sandwiches just before serving time using a serrated knife. Slice each sandwich into desired shape.

Tea Sandwich Shapes

For fingers, slice each sandwich straight through the center, then once again through each half, creating four fingers. Arrange like a starburst on a large round platter. Place cut side up so the filling is visible.

For triangles, slice each sandwich straight through the diagonals, forming four triangles. Arrange in a circle on a large round platter with the point of the cut facing up.

For squares, slice each sandwich into four squares. Arrange neatly stacked, slightly offset, on a large square or rectangular platter.

Almond Ham Filling

Yield: 1^1/2 cups

Flavorful and crunchy, this filling satisfies the requirements of great taste and full-bodied texture.

> 1 cup ground cooked ham (about ^{1}/2 pound before grinding)
> ^{1}/2 cup finely chopped almonds, toasted
> ^{1}/2 cup mayonnaise
> 2^1/2 teaspoons creamy horseradish, or to taste
> 1 hard-cooked egg, peeled and finely chopped
> 2 tablespoons finely chopped fresh parsley (optional)

Combine the ham, almonds, mayonnaise, horseradish, egg and parsley in a bowl and mix well. Garnish the sandwiches with fresh parsley sprigs.

Corned Beef and Horseradish Filling

Yield: 2 cups

Be sure to use old-fashioned horseradish found in the refrigerator section of your grocery store when making this teatime favorite, introduced over four decades ago at the Restaurant.

> 1 (12-ounce) can corned beef, fat removed and beef chopped
> 1 tablespoon prepared horseradish
> 3 tablespoons sour cream
> ^{1}/2 large dill pickle, chopped

Combine the corned beef, horseradish, sour cream and pickle in a food processor fitted with a steel blade. Pulse until the mixture has reached spreading consistency.

Eight Fancy Tea Sandwiches

For eight fancy tops, trim crusts from one slice of white bread and one slice of dark bread. Cut each slice into four squares, creating four white and four dark squares.

With a cookie cutter, cut desired shape (such as circles, hearts, spades, and so forth) out of each square.

Pull the desired shape out of each frame. You will have four dark-colored shapes and four white ones. Replace the dark-colored shapes inside the white frames and the white-colored shapes inside the dark frames. You now have eight fancy tops for eight tea sandwiches.

To assemble, spread two slices bread with desired filling. Trim crusts from each slice and cut into eight squares. Cover with eight fancy tops. Arrange on a large rectangular platter.

Garnishes

Use small sprigs of fresh herbs such as parsley or dill to decorate tops. Use larger sprigs of herbs or edible flowers to garnish the serving plate. Dip one side of triangles in finely minced fresh parsley and stand parsley-coated side up. Don't forget paper doilies.

Hot Artichoke Parmesan Squares

Yield: 32 squares

Tempting and luscious! Watch them disappear.

> ^{1}/$_2$ cup drained and mashed water-packed artichoke bottoms
> 1 teaspoon seeded and minced jalapeño chile (use more for a spicier taste)
> 1^1/$_2$ cups grated Parmesan cheese
> ^{1}/$_2$ cup mayonnaise
> ^{1}/$_2$ cup sour cream
> 2 teaspoons grated onion
> 8 slices white bread, crusts trimmed
> Paprika

Lightly grease a baking sheet. Preheat the oven to 400 degrees. Purée the artichokes and the jalapeño chile in a food processor. Combine the artichoke purée, cheese, mayonnaise, sour cream and onion in a small bowl and mix well. Adjust the seasoning to taste. Cut each slice of bread into 4 squares. Place a heaping tablespoonful of the artichoke mixture on each of the small squares, keeping the squares together. Spread the artichoke mounds evenly over the entire slice. Separate the squares and place them on the prepared baking sheet. Repeat with the remaining slices. Bake until the topping is bubbly but not browned. Sprinkle with paprika and serve hot.

Parmesan Twists

Yield: about 30 twists

Everyone will beg for seconds of this rich, flaky strip made with puff pastry and spiked with salty herbs.

> 1 sheet puff pastry, thawed
> 2 egg yolks
> 4 teaspoons water
> 1 cup grated Parmesan cheese
> 1 teaspoon paprika
> ^{1}/$_4$ teaspoon Italian herbs, or to taste
> 1 teaspoon coarse salt

Grease a large baking sheet. Preheat the oven to 400 degrees. Roll the pastry sheet into a ^{1}/$_8$-inch-thick rectangle on a lightly floured surface. Beat the egg yolks and water in a small bowl. Brush the pastry sheet with ^{1}/$_2$ of the egg yolk mixture. Sprinkle the cheese lengthwise over ^{1}/$_2$ of the pastry. Fold the unspread half over the cheese and press to seal the edges. Roll the pastry lightly until the short side is 5 inches in length. Cut the pastry into ^{1}/$_2$×5-inch strips. Twist each strip loosely and brush with the remaining egg mixture. Combine the paprika, herbs and salt. Sprinkle over the twisted strips. Place ^{1}/$_2$ inch apart on the prepared baking sheet. Bake for 12 to 15 minutes or until golden brown. Serve hot or at room temperature.

Prosciutto Crisps

Yield: 18 to 36 crisps

A base of flaky puff pastry is rolled around a honey-mustard prosciutto filling. These crisps are a must for that special cocktail party or afternoon tea. Assemble the rolls ahead and chill them for several hours, or freeze and thaw before completing.

1 sheet puff pastry, thawed
1 tablespoon honey
1 tablespoon Dijon mustard
1/4 teaspoon prepared horseradish
2 tablespoons grated Parmesan cheese
3 ounces thinly sliced prosciutto
1 egg yolk
2 teaspoons water

Arrange the pastry sheet on a lightly floured surface. Combine the honey, Dijon mustard and horseradish in a small bowl and mix to form a smooth paste. Spread over the pastry. Layer the cheese and prosciutto over the pastry. Roll as for a jelly roll from the long side, stopping at the middle. Roll the opposite side toward the middle, forming two side-by-side pinwheels. Wrap the double roll in plastic wrap and place on a flat baking sheet. Chill for several hours or freeze for up to 3 weeks. Thaw the frozen roll for 8 hours in the refrigerator before proceeding.

Line 2 baking sheets with parchment paper. Preheat the oven to 400 degrees. Cut the roll into 1/4- to 1/2-inch-thick slices, using a serrated knife. Place the slices 1 inch apart on the prepared baking sheet. Beat the egg yolk and water in a small bowl and brush over the slices. Bake for 10 to 12 minutes or until golden. Serve hot or at room temperature.

Teatime on Cervantes Court

Caraway Squares

Yield: about 40 squares

Afternoon tea would not be complete without this crunchy morsel made with puff pastry, embedded with shredded Gouda or Swiss cheese and just a hint of nutmeg.

1 sheet puff pastry, thawed
1 egg yolk
2 teaspoons water
1 cup (4 ounces) shredded Gouda or Swiss cheese
3 to 4 teaspoons caraway seeds
$1/8$ teaspoon sugar
$1/8$ teaspoon nutmeg

Grease a large baking sheet. Preheat the oven to 400 degrees. Roll the pastry sheet into a $1/8$-inch-thick rectangle. Beat the egg yolk and water in a small bowl and brush over the pastry. Combine the cheese, caraway seeds, sugar and nutmeg in a small bowl and mix well. Sprinkle over the pastry. Roll lightly with a rolling pin over the cheese and seeds, embedding them in the pastry. Cut into 2-inch squares. Place $1/2$ inch apart on the prepared baking sheet. Bake for 10 to 12 minutes or until golden brown. Serve hot or at room temperature.

Chèvre Cheese Rounds

Yield: 96 to 100 rounds

Serve this dual-purpose crispy bread morsel as a canapé or as a garnish for a salad.

1 pound plain chèvre, softened
1 tablespoon chopped fresh chives
$1/4$ teaspoon tarragon
$1/8$ teaspoon thyme
$1/8$ teaspoon garlic powder
20 slices white bread, cut into $11/2$-inch rounds
Balsamic vinegar

Preheat the broiler. Grease a large baking sheet. Combine the chèvre, chives, tarragon, thyme and garlic powder in a small bowl and mix until smooth. Broil the bread rounds until toasted on one side. Brush vinegar on the untoasted side. Spread a little of the cheese mixture on each round and place the rounds on the prepared pan. Broil until the cheese is bubbly. Serve hot.

Cheese Pillows

Yield: 50 servings

A decades-old tea favorite at the Restaurant. These light-as-a-cloud puffs will surely satisfy bread and cheese lovers. Make them ahead and have on hand in the freezer when company arrives.

> 1 cup (4 ounces) shredded Cheddar cheese or Swiss cheese
> 3 ounces cream cheese
> 1/2 cup (1 stick) butter
> 1/2 teaspoon minced garlic
> 1/4 teaspoon cayenne pepper
> 2 egg whites, stiffly beaten
> 1 loaf French bread, or 1/2 pound unsliced white bread or
>   Pullman loaf, slightly stale, crusts trimmed and cut into
>   1-inch cubes

Grease a baking sheet that will fit in your freezer. Combine the Cheddar cheese, cream cheese, butter and garlic in a nonstick saucepan over medium-low heat. Stir until the cheeses and butter melt. Add the cayenne pepper. Remove from the heat and let cool slightly. Fold the beaten egg whites gently into the cheese mixture. Dip each bread cube in the mixture, coating well. Place on the prepared baking sheet and place the sheet in the freezer. Remove the frozen cubes to a freezer bag and store in the freezer until ready to use.

Grease a large baking sheet. Preheat the oven to 400 degrees. Place the desired number of frozen squares on the prepared sheet. Bake for 8 to 10 minutes or until lightly browned. Serve hot or at room temperature. Reheat squares that have cooled in a 300-degree oven, if desired.

Pullman Loaf, aka Pain de Mie

Pain de mie (Pullman loaf) is a classic French white bread with a fine yet compact texture. It is the best base for making perfectly shaped, uniform hors d'oeuvres or canapés because it is easy to slice evenly. It is baked in a rectangular pan (Pullman pan) with a sliding lid that is closed while the bread bakes, compressing the dough into a perfect rectangle and making the bread dense.

It can be ordered from the bakery. However, if you choose to bake this yourself and cannot find a Pullman pan, which measures 3 1/2 × 3 1/2 × 16, you can use a loaf pan that has similar dimensions. For the lid, you can place a baking sheet over the dough, and place six pounds or more of an ovenproof weight, such as a cast-iron skillet, on the top. This bread freezes beautifully, double wrapped, for two to three weeks.

Spicy Surprise Puffs

Yield: 5 dozen puffs

A rich and flaky bite-size pastry ball is neatly shaped around a surprise: a pimento-stuffed olive.

2 cups (8 ounces) shredded sharp Cheddar
   cheese, softened
1/4 cup grated Parmesan cheese
6 tablespoons butter, softened
1 tablespoon Worcestershire sauce
1 teaspoon dry mustard

1/2 teaspoon paprika
1/4 teaspoon salt
1/4 teaspoon cayenne pepper
3/4 cup all-purpose flour
1 (10-ounce) jar pimento-stuffed green olives,
   drained (about 60 small olives)

Combine the Cheddar cheese, Parmesan cheese and butter in a food processor or the bowl of an electric mixer and process until smooth. Add the Worcestershire sauce, dry mustard, paprika, salt and cayenne pepper and process until well combined. Stir in the flour gradually. Chill the dough for 30 minutes.

Preheat the oven to 400 degrees. Shape the dough by teaspoonfuls into balls. Flatten each ball into a circle. Place an olive in the center and press the dough around the olive to form a ball. Roll each ball in your hand to smooth the surface. Place the balls in muffin cups or 2 inches apart on a baking sheet. Bake for 10 to 12 minutes or until lightly browned. Serve hot or at room temperature.

Miniature Chile Frittatas

Yield: about 40 servings

Full of southwestern flavor, these tiny crustless quiches will be popular with low-carb dieters.
They are equally good served hot or cold.

1 cup small curd cottage cheese
5 eggs, beaten
1/4 cup all-purpose flour
1/8 teaspoon cayenne pepper, or to taste
1/4 teaspoon salt
1/4 cup (1/2 stick) butter, melted

2 (4-ounce) cans diced mild green chiles,
   drained
2 cups (8 ounces) shredded Monterey Jack
   cheese or a mixture of Monterey Jack cheese
   and Cheddar cheese
1/2 teaspoon baking powder

Blend the cottage cheese in a food processor or mixer until smooth. Add the eggs, flour, cayenne pepper and salt. Beat until well blended. Stir in the butter, chiles and cheese. Chill, covered, for 2 to 24 hours before baking. Grease 1 3/4-inch muffin cups. Preheat the oven to 350 degrees. Add the baking powder to the chilled mixture and mix well. Spoon 1 tablespoonful into each muffin cup. Bake for 15 to 20 minutes or until puffed and golden brown. Let stand until slightly cool; run a sharp knife around each frittata to loosen. Serve hot or at room temperature. Bake the frittatas ahead, if desired. Cool completely and wrap tightly. Chill in the refrigerator until ready to serve. Reheat in a preheated 350-degree oven for 5 to 8 minutes.

Bite-Size Crab Quiches

Yield: 36 servings

Crab is flavored with a hint of curry in these little quiches. Whenever a recipe in this book calls for a piecrust, we recommend the easy, no-fail Cream Cheese Crust featured with this recipe. It's almost as quick to make as opening a package.

$^1/_2$ pound crab meat, drained and flaked, or 2 (6-ounce) cans crab meat,
　　drained and flaked
1 cup (4 ounces) shredded Swiss cheese or sharp Cheddar cheese
$^1/_2$ cup mayonnaise
2 tablespoons chopped green onions
1 tablespoon finely chopped red or green bell pepper
1 teaspoon fresh lemon juice
$^1/_2$ teaspoon curry powder
1 recipe Cream Cheese Crust

Combine the crab meat, cheese, mayonnaise, green onions, bell pepper, lemon juice and curry powder in a bowl and mix well. Chill the mixture while preparing the Cream Cheese Crust. Preheat the oven to 400 degrees. Roll the dough $^1/_8$ inch thick on a floured surface. Cut into 2-inch rounds. Press each round on the bottom and up the side of 36 miniature muffin cups. Spoon the crab meat filling evenly into the cups. Bake on the lowest oven rack for 15 minutes or until golden brown. Serve hot.

Cream Cheese Crust

Yield: 1 (9-inch) piecrust or 36 tartlet shells

This is a fail-proof piecrust that does not require prebaking.

$^1/_2$ cup (1 stick) butter, chilled
3 ounces cream cheese, chilled
1 cup all-purpose flour

Combine the butter and cream cheese in a food processor fitted with a steel blade and process until smooth. Add the flour and pulse just until blended. Shape the dough into a smooth round on a sheet of plastic wrap. Bring the plastic wrap around the dough to wrap tightly. Chill for 1 hour or until ready to bake. Let stand at room temperature for a few minutes before rolling.

Asparagus Roll-Ups

Yield: 75 servings

This is one of the oldest tea recipes served at the Restaurant and still remains a favorite. The rolls require freezing before cutting, baking, and serving.

25 fresh asparagus spears, peeled
8 ounces cream cheese, softened
4 ounces blue cheese, softened
1 egg
1/2 teaspoon garlic salt
25 thin soft white bread slices,
    crusts trimmed
1 1/2 cups (3 sticks) butter, melted

Trim both ends of each asparagus spear to the length of a bread slice, reserving the tips for another use. Cook the asparagus in boiling salted water in a saucepan for 2 to 4 minutes or until tender. Drain and plunge the asparagus into ice water to stop the cooking process; drain and dry well. Grease a large baking sheet. Combine the cream cheese, blue cheese, egg and garlic salt in a small bowl and mix well. Roll the bread slices flat with a rolling pin. Spread each slice with the cheese mixture and place an asparagus spear on the lower 1/3 of each slice. Roll up the bread around the asparagus. Brush each roll with the butter, coating all sides. Place the rolls seam side down on the prepared baking sheet and freeze until ready to bake. Preheat the oven to 400 degrees. Cut the frozen rolls into thirds. Bake while still frozen for 15 minutes or until lightly browned. Serve warm.

The Craftsman
Ribbon reads, "And by knowledge shall the chambers be filled with all precious and pleasant riches."

Belgian Endive Boats

Yield: 20 servings

For an elegant appetizer, arrange these "boats" like a sunburst on a bed of red leaf lettuce.

6 ounces (about) Belgian endive
4 ounces cream cheese, softened
1 tablespoon freshly grated Parmesan cheese
2 teaspoons chili sauce
1 tablespoon minced cilantro
1/4 teaspoon dry mustard
1/4 teaspoon Worcestershire sauce
1/8 teaspoon salt, or to taste
1/8 teaspoon pepper, or to taste
60 peeled cooked baby shrimp
Red leaf lettuce leaves

Remove 20 outer leaves from the endive, reserving the remainder for another use. Rinse and dry the leaves; wrap them in towels. Chill the leaves until ready to assemble. Combine the cream cheese, Parmesan cheese, chili sauce, cilantro, dry mustard, Worcestershire sauce, salt and pepper in a bowl and mix well. Chill until ready to assemble. Spoon or pipe about 2 teaspoons of the cheese mixture down the center of each endive leaf. Top each with 3 baby shrimp. Remove to a serving tray lined with red leaf lettuce. Serve immediately.

Survival of the Teas

Tea service gradually grew to a maximum of about one hundred guests per day. Unfortunately, over time, cultural changes affected the duration of the tea service. More and more women were working full-time jobs just to make ends meet. All of a sudden, women no longer had the luxury of time to enjoy afternoon tea. Numbers gradually diminished to the point where tea service was no longer economical on a daily basis.

Daily tea service was discontinued in 1980. However, the Valentine's Tea and the Holiday Tea continued to thrive. The number of guests for each of these annual teas increased to over two hundred, requiring two seatings for each event. The demand for reservations always exceeded available seats. Local choirs often performed at the Holiday Tea. Fire regulations eventually ended the choir program, but did not end the popularity of the teas.

Watercress Tomato Roulade

Yield: 18 to 20 servings

A colorful filling of cream cheese, tomatoes, and basil is rolled jelly roll fashion in a soufflé-type watercress base for a great appetizer or a light first course. The roll should be chilled for two to four hours before slicing and serving.

Watercress Roulade Base
2 egg yolks
1 bunch watercress, leaves only, washed, dried and finely chopped
2 tablespoons finely chopped fresh parsley
2 tablespoons grated Parmesan cheese
1/2 teaspoon salt
1/8 teaspoon pepper
2 egg whites, stiffly beaten

Filling
8 ounces cream cheese, softened
2 tablespoons milk
1/2 teaspoon salt
1/8 teaspoon pepper
2 firm Roma tomatoes, peeled, seeded, finely chopped and drained
1 1/2 tablespoons chopped fresh basil leaves

For the watercress roulade, line a jelly roll pan with parchment paper; grease the parchment paper. Preheat the oven to 375 degrees. Beat the egg yolks in a large bowl until thick and pale yellow. Fold in the watercress, parsley, cheese, salt and pepper. Fold the beaten egg whites gently into the watercress mixture. Spread the batter into an 8×14-inch rectangle in the prepared pan. Bake for 10 to 12 minutes, being careful not to brown. Cool on the parchment paper. Chill, covered, for up to 1 day.

For the filling, line a baking sheet with waxed paper. Combine the cream cheese, milk, salt and pepper in a small bowl and mix well. Spread in a thin layer to the edge of the watercress base. Arrange the tomatoes over the cream cheese filling and sprinkle with the basil. Roll as for a jelly roll from the long side. Place seam side down on the prepared baking sheet. Chill, covered, for 2 hours or until firm. Trim the ends and cut the log into 1/2- to 3/4-inch slices.

Spiced Pecans

Yield: 2 pounds

This versatile treat is great to have on hand for snacking or to add to salads or desserts. Make extras to give as hostess or holiday gifts.

1 tablespoon salt
2 teaspoons cinnamon
2 teaspoons nutmeg
1 teaspoon ginger
3/4 teaspoon ground cloves
1/4 teaspoon ground allspice
1/2 teaspoon cayenne pepper
3 egg whites
1 1/2 cups granulated sugar or packed brown sugar
1/3 cup dry sherry or port
8 cups pecan halves

Grease 2 large baking sheets with shallow sides. Preheat the oven to 250 degrees. Combine the salt, cinnamon, nutmeg, ginger, cloves, allspice and cayenne pepper in a small bowl and mix well; divide the mixture in half. Beat the egg whites in a large bowl until stiff peaks form. Add 1/2 of the spice mixture, sugar and sherry. Beat until well blended. Add the pecans and stir to coat well. Drain the nuts in a colander set over a bowl for 15 minutes; discard the drained liquid. Return the nuts to the mixing bowl and sprinkle with the remaining spice mixture, stirring to coat evenly. Spread the nuts in a single layer in the prepared baking sheets. Bake for 1 hour and 20 minutes to 1 1/2 hours or until the nuts are dry and lightly browned, stirring every 10 minutes. Use chopsticks to separate the nuts if necessary. Rotate the baking sheets if your oven does not cook evenly. Cool completely. Store in airtight containers at room temperature or in the freezer. Serve frozen nuts directly from the freezer.

Blue Garden

Breads, Spreads and Dips

Bunny Days

Almost no menu-planning chore is more difficult than the one facing Auxiliary members during the week of Bunny Days. Not only do they have to create a menu that pleases more than five hundred picky-eating, over-stimulated toddlers, they also have to devise a grown-up menu for the parents. In addition to that, one of the days is Good Friday, with its meatless restrictions for many customers. You can begin to appreciate the difficulties facing the menu planners.

In past years, cooks slaved over such gourmet kid foods as pear bunnies with elaborate faces and tiny sandwiches cut into a variety of animal shapes. It soon became apparent, however, that children were too excited to eat much more than a carrot curl or two and maybe some finger Jell-o bunnies. Consequently, lunches became simpler. In recent years, macaroni and cheese has become a modest hit with the kids, especially when followed by Easter baskets filled with homemade cookies, a big chocolate egg donated by See's Candy, and a package of Jelly Bellies donated by Jelly Belly Candies.

Adults, meanwhile, enjoy a proper lunch consisting of a starter, followed by a hot entrée, Signature Rolls, dessert, and a hot or cold beverage. When the "Bunny" (an intrepid volunteer who seriously takes on this job each year) enters the room, all semblance of order disappears. The Bunny distributes balloons to shrieks of both fear and delight while the grown-ups finish their dessert and coffee. Pandemonium definitely rules.

Eventually, the dining room empties as all guests, young and old, adjourn to the patio for pictures with the Bunny. The only reminders of the previous disorder are the balloons on the ceiling and the finger Jell-o bunnies on the floor. There would certainly be no mistaking a Bunny Day for, say, a Valentine's Day Tea.

The Allied Arts Guild Restaurant
Welcomes You to

Bunny Days

Adult Menu

Zucchini Bisque Delight

Tomato Herbed Fish Fillets
Served in a Ramekin, with Lemon Wedge

Lemon Dill Rice

Fresh Steamed Broccoli Florets

Signature Rolls and Butter

Orange Cheesecake Flan

Coffee, Tea, Lemonade

Children's Menu

Creamy Macaroni and Cheese

Carrot Sticks and Bunches of
Red and White Grapes on a Bed of Shredded Lettuce

Easter Basket Filled with
See's Chocolate Eggs, Jelly Belly Candies, Swedish Ginger Cookie Bunnies

Lemonade, Milk

Entrance of the Easter Bunny Passing Out Balloons

On the Patio

Pictures with the Easter Bunny

Benefiting Lucile Packard Children's Hospital at Stanford

Signature Rolls

Yield: 4 to 5 dozen petite rolls

Baked daily in the Restaurant's kitchen since 1979, these soft, buttery rolls became a welcome accompaniment to our luncheons. They require at least three hours' rising time.

$1/2$ cup sugar
1 cup lukewarm (110- to 115-degree) water
1 envelope dry yeast
$1/2$ cup (1 stick) butter, melted and cooled
3 eggs
1 teaspoon salt
$41/2$ to 5 cups all-purpose flour
$1/4$ cup ($1/2$ stick) butter, melted

Dissolve 1 teaspoon of the sugar in the water in a small bowl. Sprinkle the yeast over the water and stir to dissolve. Let stand for 5 to 10 minutes or until the yeast begins to bubble. Combine $1/2$ cup butter, eggs and yeast mixture in the large bowl of an electric mixer fitted with a beater paddle. Beat until well combined. Combine the remaining sugar, salt and $41/2$ cups flour in a bowl. Add to the egg mixture and beat well. Add more flour, 1 tablespoon at a time, until the dough pulls away from side of the bowl and is soft and slightly moist. Place the dough in a large greased bowl, turning to coat the surface. Let rise, covered, in the refrigerator for at least 3 hours, but preferably 8 hours.

Let the dough stand at room temperature for 30 minutes. Grease a baking sheet with sides. Roll the dough $3/4$ to 1 inch thick on a lightly floured surface. Cut with a 1-inch biscuit cutter dipped in flour, cutting close to the edges of the dough and to previous cuts to minimize scraps. Knead the scraps of dough together and cut remaining rolls. Place the rolls almost touching on the prepared baking sheet. Let rise, covered, in a warm place for 1 hour or until doubled in bulk. Preheat the oven to 400 degrees while the rolls are rising. Bake for 12 minutes or until golden brown. Brush the tops with melted butter. Serve warm.

Those Darling Little Rolls

Over the years, many types of breads have been tried at the Restaurant. Nut bread with cream cheese was served with fruit salads. Poppy seed rolls were served with entrées. Hot cross buns were offered during the Easter season. At other times of the year, for the sake of variety, bran muffins were introduced.

However, the most popular bread by far has been our Signature Rolls. Repeat customers came to expect these petite rolls on a daily basis without fail. At first we bought them from local bakeries, but then resigned ourselves to producing them in our own kitchen.

No matter what other types of wonderful luncheon breads we introduced over the years, when we did serve something new, we always heard the same disappointed query from our guests, "Where are those darling little rolls?"

Consequently, realizing the desires of our repeat customers, and understanding the role of our rolls within the eyes of the community, "those darling little rolls" became the signature item of the Restaurant.

Swedish Limpa Bread

Yield: 2 loaves

Scented with orange, this traditional Christmas rye bread will become a favorite in your home. Serve it simply with butter or with one of our delicious spreads. The bread requires at least three hours' rising time.

1 envelope dry yeast
1/2 cup lukewarm (110- to 115-degree) water
2 cups rye flour
2 cups lukewarm (110- to 115-degree) water
1/2 cup dark molasses
1/4 cup sugar
1/4 cup vegetable oil
2 teaspoons caraway seeds
1 teaspoon anise extract
1 1/2 teaspoons salt
Grated zest of 1 orange
4 1/2 to 5 1/2 cups all-purpose flour
2 tablespoons butter, melted

Dissolve the yeast in 1/2 cup water in a small bowl. Combine the rye flour and 2 cups water in a large bowl and mix well. Stir in the molasses, sugar, oil, caraway seeds, anise extract, salt and orange zest. Add the yeast mixture and stir well. Stir in enough of the flour to make a soft dough. Let rise, covered, in a warm place until doubled in bulk.

Grease two 2 1/2-quart round casseroles. Knead the dough on a floured surface until smooth and elastic, adding additional flour as needed. Divide the dough into halves and shape into 2 round loaves. Place in the prepared casseroles. Prick the top of the dough with a fork. Let rise, covered, in a warm place for 1 hour or until doubled in bulk. Preheat the oven to 375 degrees while the loaves are rising. Bake for 40 minutes or until the loaves pull away from the side of the casserole and sound hollow when tapped. Cover the tops with foil partway through cooking if they are browning too rapidly. Cool on a wire rack. Brush the warm loaves with the melted butter. Serve warm or at room temperature. Reheat in a 350-degree oven for 10 to 15 minutes, if desired.

Working with Yeast

After years of experience making Signature Rolls at the Restaurant, the volunteers have found the following tips to be helpful when making yeast breads.

First, always check the expiration date of the yeast to ensure its viability. Have all ingredients and utensils at room temperature before mixing the dough. Allow the dough to rise in a warm, draft-free place before baking.

In the Restaurant, pans of rolls are always placed on bakers' racks close to the ovens. At home, the oven, warmed at its lowest setting for one minute and then turned off, offers a convenient place. When dough has doubled in size, test completion of the rise by inserting a finger in the dough. If a dent remains, proceed with the next step.

Freezing Breads

When you plan to freeze rolls or bread, first cool completely. Then wrap in foil and enclose in a plastic freezer bag. Thaw at room temperature while still wrapped and then reheat in foil until warm.

Cheese Bread

Yield: 1 loaf

Quick, easy, and versatile, this savory bread is great for breakfast or served with soups and salads.

> 1³/4 cups all-purpose flour
> 1 cup (4 ounces) shredded Cheddar cheese
> ¹/4 cup sugar
> 2¹/2 teaspoons baking powder
> 1¹/2 teaspoons dried dillweed
> 1 teaspoon dried onion flakes
> ³/4 teaspoon salt
> 1 egg, beaten
> ³/4 cup milk
> ¹/3 cup vegetable oil

Spray a 5×9-inch loaf pan with nonstick cooking spray. Preheat the oven to 400 degrees. Combine the flour, cheese, sugar, baking powder, dillweed, onion flakes and salt in a medium bowl. Beat the egg with the milk and oil in a large bowl. Add the dry ingredients and stir just until mixed. Pour into the prepared pan. Bake for 35 minutes or until the loaf tests done. Serve warm.

Pumpkin Bread

Yield: 1 large loaf or 4 small loaves

A favorite family recipe passed through the generations, this spice-filled bread boasts a unique characteristic: no eggs. Bake the batter in miniature loaf pans for a great giveaway treat.

> 2¹/2 cups all-purpose flour
> 4 teaspoons baking soda
> ¹/2 teaspoon cinnamon
> ¹/2 teaspoon ground cloves
> ¹/4 teaspoon nutmeg
> ¹/2 teaspoon salt
> 1 (15-ounce) can pumpkin
> 2 cups sugar
> ¹/2 cup vegetable oil
> 1 cup chopped walnuts
> ¹/2 cup raisins (optional)

Grease a 5×9-inch loaf pan or 4 miniature pans. Preheat the oven to 350 degrees. Combine the flour, baking soda, cinnamon, cloves, nutmeg and salt in a large bowl. Combine the pumpkin, sugar and oil in a medium bowl and mix well. Add to the dry ingredients and stir just until mixed. Stir in the walnuts and raisins. Fill the prepared pans ³/4 full. Bake the large loaf for 1 hour or until the loaf tests done. Bake the small loaves for 35 to 40 minutes or until they test done. Cool completely before slicing.

Breads for Fillings and Spreads

Try spreading our tea sandwich fillings or our spreads on homemade Melba toast. As an alternative, fill mini-bread cups, fillo baskets, or won ton cups with a filling or a spread of your choice. Also, fill with puddings or fruit spreads.

Melba Toast

Cut thinly sliced bread of your choice or cocktail bread into desired shapes. Crusts may be left on or removed. Brush both sides with melted butter. Top with any 1 or more of the following flavorings: anise, caraway, celery seed, cumin, dill, sesame seeds, finely minced garlic, or shallots with rosemary. Bake on a greased cookie sheet in a preheated 250-degree oven for 1 hour. Cool on wire racks. Store in airtight containers. Use as a base for canapés or serve with soups or salads.

Miniature Herb Biscuits

Yield: 16 biscuits

Enhanced with fresh herbs and spices, these biscuits can be served as appetizers or as accompaniments with soups or main entrées.

2 cups all-purpose flour
2 1/2 teaspoons baking powder
1/2 teaspoon salt
1/4 teaspoon dry mustard
1/4 teaspoon black pepper
1/8 teaspoon cayenne pepper
6 tablespoons cold butter or shortening, cut into small pieces
3/4 cup plus 3 tablespoons milk
2 large green onions, minced
1 tablespoon finely chopped fresh parsley
Melted butter or milk to brush tops of biscuits

Grease a baking sheet. Preheat the oven to 400 degrees. Combine the flour, baking powder, salt, dry mustard, black pepper and cayenne pepper in a food processor. Pulse 2 or 3 times. Add the butter and pulse 10 to 15 times or until the mixture is crumbly. Add the milk, green onions and parsley; pulse just until the dough forms a soft moist ball.

Roll the dough into an 8×10-inch rectangle about 3/4 inch thick on a lightly floured board. Cut with a 2-inch biscuit cutter dipped in flour. Knead scraps of dough together and cut remaining biscuits. Place 1 inch apart on the prepared baking sheet. Brush the tops with melted butter or milk. Bake for 20 to 25 minutes or until golden brown. Serve hot.

Mini-Bread Cups

Remove crusts from white bread slices. Roll each slice paper-thin. Cut into 2-inch rounds or squares. Brush with melted butter. Insert each round or square into buttered cups of a mini-muffin tin. Bake in a preheated 375-degree oven until browned, about 5 minutes. Fill with filling of your choice.

Fillo Baskets

Brush a sheet of fillo dough with melted butter. Cut into 3-inch squares. Butter the cups of a nonstick mini-muffin tin. Line each cup with a square of fillo. Top each square with 2 or 3 additional squares, orienting each square so that points are staggered for a petal-like appearance. Bake in a preheated 375-degree oven for 10 minutes or until golden. Watch carefully. Fill with filling of your choice.

Won Ton Cups

Press two 1/2-inch square won ton wrappers into buttered cups of a nonstick mini-muffin tin. Lightly spray wrappers with cooking oil. Bake in a preheated 350-degree oven for 7 to 10 minutes or until lightly browned. Remove won ton cups from pan and cool on a rack. Store in airtight containers. Cups will keep for about a month.

Ginger Scones

Yield: 8 large or 16 small scones

Small chunks of crystallized ginger combined with generous amounts of butter and fresh cream produce a pungently sweet-tasting and flaky-light confection so irresistible it begs for seconds.

3 cups all-purpose flour
6 tablespoons sugar
4 teaspoons baking powder
3/4 teaspoon salt
3/4 cup (1 1/2 sticks) cold unsalted butter, cut into small pieces
1 cup half-and-half
1 cup finely chopped crystallized ginger

Grease a baking sheet or line it with parchment paper. Preheat the oven to 400 degrees. Combine the flour, sugar, baking powder and salt in a food processor. Pulse 2 or 3 times. Add the butter and pulse 10 to 15 times or until the mixture is crumbly. Remove to a large bowl. Add the half-and-half and 3/4 cup of the crystallized ginger. Stir just until moistened. Knead on a floured surface for about 30 seconds. Shape into 1 flat round for large scones or 2 rounds for small scones, about 1 inch thick. Cut each round with a floured serrated knife into 8 wedges. Place 2 inches apart on the prepared baking sheet. Sprinkle the remaining 1/4 cup crystallized ginger over the tops. Bake on the middle rack for 15 to 20 minutes or until the scones have doubled in size, the tops are golden and the centers offer a slight resistance when touched. Serve warm. Store the cooled scones in an airtight container for up to 2 days.

Orange Pecan Scones

Yield: 12 scones

One bite and you will be captive forever. These scones are similar to dropped biscuits—only a whole lot better!

Easter Bunny and Friend

1$3/4$ cups all-purpose flour
1$1/2$ teaspoons baking powder
$1/2$ teaspoon baking soda
$1/3$ cup sugar
Grated zest of 1 orange
$1/2$ cup cold butter, cut into small pieces
$1/4$ cup chopped pecans
$1/4$ cup currants
$1/2$ cup orange juice
1 egg, beaten
1 tablespoon sugar
1 teaspoon grated orange zest

Grease a baking sheet. Preheat the oven to 375 degrees. Combine the flour, baking powder, baking soda, $1/3$ cup sugar and zest of 1 orange in a food processor. Pulse 2 or 3 times. Add the butter and pulse 10 to 15 times or until the mixture is crumbly. Remove to a large bowl. Stir in the pecans and currants. Combine the orange juice and egg and add to the flour mixture, stirring just until moistened. Drop the dough in 12 mounds on the prepared baking sheet. Combine 1 tablespoon sugar and 1 teaspoon orange zest and sprinkle over the scones. Bake for 12 to 15 minutes or until the scones have doubled in size, the tops are golden and the centers offer a slight resistance when touched. Serve warm.

Spicy Banana Muffins

Yield: 12 large muffins

Put your ripe bananas to good use in these tender muffins that stay moist for days. Cinnamon enhances the banana flavor.

    1 cup sugar
    1/2 cup (1 stick) butter, softened
    3 ripe bananas, finely chopped (11/2 cups)
    2 eggs, beaten
    11/4 cups all-purpose flour
    1 teaspoon baking soda
    1/4 teaspoon salt
    1/4 teaspoon cinnamon

Butter 12 muffin cups. Preheat the oven to 375 degrees. Cream the sugar and butter in a mixing bowl until light and fluffy. Stir in the bananas and eggs. Combine the flour, baking soda, salt and cinnamon in a bowl. Add to the banana mixture and stir just until moistened. Spoon into the prepared muffin cups. Bake for 20 to 25 minutes.

Best-Ever Bran Muffins

Yield: 12 large muffins

Double the recipe, refrigerate the batter for as long as two weeks, and bake at your convenience. Everyone will enjoy the spicy molasses flavor of this nutritional treat.

    11/2 cups all-bran cereal
    1/2 cup boiling water
    1 egg, slightly beaten
    1 cup buttermilk
    1/4 cup vegetable oil
    1/4 cup light molasses
    1/2 cup raisins or currants (optional)
    11/4 cups all-purpose flour
    11/4 teaspoons baking soda
    1/4 cup sugar
    1/4 teaspoon salt
    1/4 teaspoon allspice

Butter 12 muffin cups. Preheat the oven to 400 degrees. Combine the all-bran cereal with the water in a large mixing bowl, stirring to moisten. Let stand for 5 minutes. Combine the egg, buttermilk, oil, molasses and raisins. Add to the cereal mixture and stir well. Combine the flour, baking soda, sugar, salt and allspice in a bowl. Stir into the bran mixture. Spoon into the prepared muffin cups. Bake for 15 to 20 minutes.

Festive Fruit Muffins

Yield: 18 large muffins

Complement your Sunday brunch with these unique muffins—so moist they melt in your mouth. The flavors improve the second day.

2¹/2 cups all-purpose flour
³/4 cup sugar
1 tablespoon baking powder
¹/2 teaspoon salt
1 cup sour cream
¹/3 cup milk
¹/4 cup vegetable oil
1 egg, beaten
¹/2 teaspoon lemon extract
¹/2 cup chopped toasted pecans
¹/2 cup dried cranberries
1¹/2 cups firm red seedless grapes, halved

Butter 18 muffin cups. Preheat the oven to 375 degrees. Combine the flour, sugar, baking powder and salt in a large mixing bowl. Combine the sour cream, milk, oil, egg, lemon extract, pecans and cranberries in a medium bowl and mix well. Add to the dry ingredients and stir just until mixed. Gently fold in the grapes. Spoon into the prepared muffin cups. Bake on the middle rack for 15 minutes and then on the top rack for 5 minutes or until the muffins pull away from the side and the tops are lightly browned.

Beer Cheese Balls

Yield: 2 cheese balls

What makes this spread unique is the subtle flavor of lager. You don't have to be a beer lover to love it! Chill the cheese balls for three hours before serving.

2 cups (8 ounces) shredded extra-sharp
Cheddar cheese, softened
3 ounces blue cheese, softened
3 ounces cream cheese, softened
¹/2 cup lager beer
1 teaspoon caraway seeds
1 teaspoon paprika
¹/2 teaspoon dry mustard
¹/2 cup finely chopped fresh parsley

Combine the Cheddar cheese, blue cheese and cream cheese in the large bowl of an electric mixer. Beat until smooth. Add the beer, caraway seeds, paprika and dry mustard and mix until smooth. Chill for several hours. Shape the cheese mixture into 2 balls and roll each in the parsley. Chill for at least 3 hours. Serve with crackers, melba toast or assorted cocktail breads. Shape the mixture into 1-inch balls for individual canapés, if desired.

Exotic Mushroom Pâté

Yield: 1¹/2 cups

With its refreshingly different taste, this fine quality pâté is fare fit for a king. Serve it with toast points for an elegant beginning to any occasion. Chill for three hours before serving.

¹/2 cup (1 stick) butter
¹/4 cup chopped shallots
1 large garlic clove, minced
1 pound chopped mixed mushrooms, such
    as porcini, shiitake, oyster or button
¹/4 cup chicken broth
¹/4 cup brandy, warmed
8 ounces cream cheese, softened
2 tablespoons fresh lemon juice
Salt and pepper to taste

Melt the butter in a skillet over medium-low heat. Sauté the shallots and garlic in the butter until tender. Add the mushrooms and sauté for 3 to 4 minutes. Stir in the chicken broth and brandy. Bring to a boil. Cook for 5 to 8 minutes or until the liquid has almost evaporated. Let stand until cool. Combine ³/4 of the mushroom mixture, cream cheese and lemon juice in a food processor fitted with a steel blade. Process until smooth. Remove to a bowl and stir in the remaining mushroom mixture. Add the salt and pepper. Chill for at least 3 hours. Let stand at room temperature for 1 hour before serving. Garnish with finely sliced chives or green onion tops. Add a tomato rose, if desired.

Fresco of Pottery Crafts

Hungarian Spread

Yield: 2 cups

This spread is a favorite with our customers at the holiday luncheons.

8 ounces cream cheese, softened
$^1/_2$ cup (1 stick) butter
4 ounces feta cheese, crumbled
$^1/_4$ cup sour cream
$^1/_4$ cup chopped green onions
1 tablespoon Dijon mustard
2 teaspoons Hungarian paprika
1 teaspoon caraway seeds
Additional sour cream or milk

Beat the cream cheese and butter in a large mixing bowl until smooth. Add the feta cheese, sour cream, green onions, Dijon mustard, paprika and caraway seeds and mix well. Thin with sour cream or milk to reach a spreading consistency. Serve at room temperature with crackers, rye bread or melba toast.

Liverwurst Pâté Spread

Yield: 2$^1/_2$ cups

This vintage spread with a tasty twist will generate a surprising sound of "yummmm." Chill for at least two hours before serving.

2 teaspoons olive oil
3 tablespoons finely chopped onion
$^1/_2$ pound liverwurst, cut into chunks
$^1/_2$ cup sour cream
2 tablespoons dry sherry
$^1/_2$ teaspoon cracked pepper
$^1/_4$ cup plus 1 tablespoon chopped toasted
slivered almonds

Heat the olive oil in a small skillet over medium-low heat. Sauté the onion in the olive oil until medium brown. Let stand until cool. Combine the liverwurst, sour cream, sherry and pepper in a food processor fitted with a steel blade. Process until smooth. Remove to a bowl. Add the sautéed onion and stir well. Chill for at least 2 hours. Let stand at room temperature for 30 minutes. Stir in $^1/_4$ cup of the almonds. Remove to serving bowl and garnish with the remaining 1 tablespoon almonds. Serve with crisp crackers, rye melba toast or soft pumpernickel or rye bread.

Salmon Mousse Spread

This beautiful mold, full of refreshing taste, may be sliced and served as an elegant, light luncheon entrée. It may also be spread on crackers or breads and served as a canapé. Requires four hours of refrigeration before serving.

Yield: about 6 cups or 75 to 100 canapés

1 envelope unflavored gelatin
1/4 cup cold water
1/4 cup boiling water
3/4 cup mayonnaise
2 tablespoons fresh lemon juice
2 tablespoons finely chopped fresh dillweed, or 2 teaspoons dried dillweed
1 tablespoon finely minced green onions (white part only)
1/8 teaspoon Tabasco sauce
1 teaspoon salt
1/2 teaspoon prepared horseradish
1/2 teaspoon paprika
2 cups finely flaked cooked salmon or smoked salmon (non-lox type) or crab meat
3/4 cup heavy whipping cream

Coat a 6-cup decorative mold with nonstick cooking spray. Soften the gelatin in the cold water in a large mixing bowl. Add the boiling water and stir until dissolved. Cool to room temperature. Fold in the mayonnaise, lemon juice, dillweed, green onions, Tabasco sauce, salt, horseradish and paprika. Chill for 15 minutes or until partially set. Fold in the salmon. Whip the cream in a mixing bowl until stiff peaks form. Fold into the salmon mixture. Pour into the prepared mold. Chill for 4 to 8 hours. Unmold onto a serving platter. Garnish with cucumber rounds and sprigs of fresh dillweed. Serve with water crackers or assorted cocktail breads.

Roasted Garlic Dip

Yield: 2²/3 cups

Forty cloves of garlic sounds like a lot! Roasting, however, transforms the flavor into a sweet and mellow bouquet.

40 garlic cloves, peeled
1/4 cup olive oil
1 cup mayonnaise
1 cup sour cream
2 teaspoons Worcestershire sauce
1 1/2 teaspoons Dijon mustard
1 1/2 cups slivered blanched almonds, toasted and coarsely
    chopped
1/3 cup finely chopped fresh Italian parsley
2 teaspoons chopped fresh rosemary
1/4 teaspoon Tabasco sauce
Salt and pepper to taste

Preheat the oven to 300 degrees. Toss the garlic cloves with the olive oil in a small baking pan. Bake on the lowest rack for 30 minutes or until soft and golden. Let stand until cool. Combine the garlic, mayonnaise, sour cream, Worcestershire sauce and Dijon mustard in a food processor and process until the garlic is finely chopped. Remove to a mixing bowl. Stir in the almonds, parsley, rosemary and Tabasco sauce. Season with salt and pepper. Chill for at least 1 hour. Adjust the seasoning. Let stand at room temperature for 1 hour before serving. Serve with unflavored crackers, such as water crackers, or an assortment of fresh vegetables.

Undressing Cloves of Garlic

There are several ways to loosen garlic peels.

Some people microwave them on High for fifteen seconds and then peel the cloves when they have cooled.

Other people drop the unpeeled cloves into boiling water for one minute and then drain and peel when the cloves have cooled enough to handle.

Still others slice the root end off each garlic clove and then put the blade of a chef's knife over the clove and hit the knife with the heel of the hand.

We, however, think all the above methods simply complicate the procedure. At Allied Arts Guild Restaurant, volunteers have always undressed each and every clove of garlic with tender loving care the old-fashioned way...by hand!

Hot Crab Cocktail Dip

Yield: 1¹/3 cups

A hint of pepper enhances the delicate flavor of crab.

¹/2 pound fresh crab meat, or 2 (6-ounce) cans
  crab meat, drained
8 ounces cream cheese, softened
2 teaspoons Worcestershire sauce, or 1 tablespoon dry sherry
  or dry vermouth
2 tablespoons chopped green onions
1 tablespoon milk
1 teaspoon lemon juice
¹/4 teaspoon cayenne pepper

Grease a 1-quart casserole. Preheat the oven to 350 degrees. Combine the crab meat, cream cheese, Worcestershire sauce, green onions, milk, lemon juice and cayenne pepper in a bowl and mix well. Spoon into the prepared casserole. Bake for 15 minutes or microwave on High for 2 to 4 minutes or until heated through. Serve with crackers or bread cubes.

Chile Dip

Yield: 4 cups

This spicy dip is one of the Restaurant's classic appetizers.

16 ounces cream cheese, softened
1 (4-ounce) can mild or medium-hot diced green
  chiles, drained
1 (15-ounce) can stewed tomatoes, drained

Combine the cream cheese, green chiles and tomatoes in a food processor fitted with a steel blade. Process until smooth. Chill until serving time. Serve with crackers or assorted vegetables.

Quick Curry Dip

Yield: 1¹/₂ cups

Here is a fast and easy way to liven up your vegetable tray.

1¹/₂ cups mayonnaise
1 tablespoon grated onion
2 teaspoons curry powder
¹/₂ teaspoon dry mustard
¹/₂ teaspoon garlic salt
¹/₄ teaspoon lemon pepper
¹/₈ teaspoon Tabasco sauce

Combine the mayonnaise, grated onion, curry powder, dry mustard, garlic salt, lemon pepper and Tabasco sauce in a small bowl and mix well. Chill, covered, for 2 hours. Serve with fresh vegetables, such as broccoli, cauliflower, carrots or cherry tomatoes.

Ginger Dip

Yield: 1¹/₂ cups

This dip is a Restaurant favorite during the holidays, often replacing the traditional first course of soup or salad.

¹/₂ cup low-fat cottage cheese
1¹/₂ teaspoons white wine vinegar
1 (4-ounce) can water chestnuts, drained and finely chopped
¹/₂ cup mayonnaise
¹/₄ cup grated onion
2 tablespoons chopped fresh parsley
1 tablespoon finely chopped crystallized ginger
1¹/₂ teaspoons soy sauce
Dash of Tabasco sauce

Combine the cottage cheese and vinegar in a food processor and process until smooth. Remove to a bowl. Stir in the water chestnuts, mayonnaise, onion, parsley, crystallized ginger, soy sauce and Tabasco sauce. Store in the refrigerator for 1 to 2 days to allow flavors to blend. Store up to 5 days. Serve with crackers or assorted vegetables.

Steve Young's Favorite Recipe

Next time you're watching football in the comfort of your home, try Steve's favorite recipe. Offer it to your guests. It's "Super Bowl" good, easy to make and very nutritious.

AMB Dip

Ann Marie Barton

1 can (11 ounces) Mexicorn, drained
1 can (15 ounces) black beans, drained
1 can (15 ounces) kidney beans, drained
2 green onions, thinly sliced
¹/₂ cup olive oil
1 cup red wine vinegar
¹/₂ teaspoon salt, or to taste
1 avocado, cubed
1 Roma tomato, cubed
Lime tortilla chips

Combine Mexicorn, black beans, kidney beans and green onions in a large bowl. Combine olive oil, vinegar and salt in a small bowl. Whisk until blended. Stir into the bean mixture. Marinate in refrigerator until chilled, stirring frequently. Just prior to serving, drain the bean mixture and place in a serving dish. Adjust salt to taste. Garnish with avocado and tomato. Serve with lime tortilla chips.

Entrance to Courtyard

Soothing Soups

Mother's Day Luncheon

The Mother's Day Luncheon and Fashion Show has been one of the longest running events on the Restaurant's spring calendar. From the very first year, it has been a huge success. This event is held annually the day before the "official" Mother's Day so it does not conflict with any family activities planned for Mom's big Sunday. The program consists of a three-course luncheon, with favors, flowers, and a fashion show by members. The day provides a rewarding experience in a glorious setting that is not available at any price anywhere else. More understandably—and this has always been a part of our tradition of success—it provides a feeling among all who attend that they are doing something good for very ill children who need help.

Always a sellout, this event often attracts as many as four generations of guests at one table. Each place is set with an envelope of complimentary recipes. The tables are decorated with vases of labeled, prize-winning roses from the Peninsula Rose Society. Teams of volunteers in colorful smocks serve the meal that the menu planning committee has been fine-tuning for weeks. It always includes a starter, followed by an entrée, our Signature Rolls, dessert, and choice of hot or cold beverages.

Attractively clad members of the Auxiliary stroll informally through the dining room and terrace modeling lovely fashions from local shops. Guests enjoy being able to converse with the models and ask questions about the various fashions in a leisurely manner. A feeling of relaxation and indulgence fills the air.

The idyllic setting, the elegant food, the gracious service, the roses, the fashions, all combine to make the Mother's Day Luncheon a gracious "thank-you" to show mothers and grandmothers how much they are loved and appreciated.

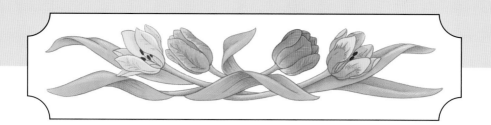

Allied Arts Guild Restaurant
Welcomes You to

Mother's Day Luncheon and Fashion Show

Menu

*Fruited Spinach Salad with Sliced Strawberries,
Spiced Pecans, Crumbled Blue Cheese and Honey Mustard Dressing*

Breast of Chicken Elegant with Mushroom White Wine Sauce

Roasted Asparagus Tips with Lemon and Parmesan Cheese

Curried Fruit

Signature Rolls with Butter

Crème Parisienne with Raspberry Sauce

Coffee, Tea, Lemonade

Complimentary Envelope of Recipes for Each Guest

Please Enjoy The Fashion Show
Featuring Fashions from Local Boutiques
Modeled by Members of The Palo Alto Auxiliary

Benefiting the Lucile Packard Children's Hospital at Stanford

Gazpacho

Yield: 9 to 10 servings

Prepare this traditional cold Spanish summer soup when tomatoes are in their prime. It's always a hit at the Restaurant. Make it ahead to allow time for the flavors to develop.

1 green bell pepper, chopped
1/2 cup chopped onion
2 large celery ribs, chopped
2 tablespoons chopped fresh parsley
2 teaspoons chopped chives
2 garlic cloves, chopped
1/4 cup red wine vinegar
3 tablespoons olive oil
2 tablespoons lemon juice
11/2 teaspoons Worcestershire sauce
1/2 teaspoon pepper
1/2 teaspoon Tabasco sauce, or to taste
1 large slice French or Italian bread, crust trimmed and cut into cubes
3 large tomatoes, peeled, seeded and chopped
1 large cucumber, peeled, seeded and chopped
41/2 cups tomato juice
Salt to taste

Process the bell pepper, onion, celery, parsley, chives, garlic, vinegar, olive oil, lemon juice, Worcestershire sauce, pepper, Tabasco sauce and bread cubes in batches in a blender until smooth. Remove to a large bowl. Stir in the tomatoes, cucumber, tomato juice and salt. Chill, covered, for up to 4 or 5 days. Serve the soup well chilled with a tray of assorted garnishes such as croutons, chopped avocado, finely chopped green onions, finely chopped red or green bell peppers, baby shrimp or chopped fresh cilantro.

Chilled Cucumber Soup

Yield: 5 servings

This soup is subtle and refreshing with a cool, clean taste. You may want to double the recipe, as everyone is sure to want seconds. Make it early in the day or a day in advance.

1/4 cup (1/2 stick) butter
2 onions, chopped
2 leeks, white parts only, sliced
2 large cucumbers, peeled, seeded and sliced
2 cups chicken broth
2 tablespoons dry white wine
1 teaspoon butter, softened
1 teaspoon all-purpose flour
1 large cucumber, peeled, seeded and cut into 1/4-inch cubes
1/2 cup heavy cream
11/2 teaspoons minced fresh dillweed, or 1/2 teaspoon dried dillweed
1 teaspoon lemon juice
5 drops of Tabasco sauce, or to taste
1 teaspoon salt, or to taste
1/2 teaspoon white pepper

Melt 1/4 cup butter in a 6-quart soup pot over low to medium heat. Sauté the onions and leeks in the butter for 10 minutes or until tender. Stir in the 2 sliced cucumbers, the chicken broth and white wine. Bring to a boil. Combine 1 teaspoon butter and the flour in a small bowl and mix well. Whisk into the soup. Reduce the heat and simmer, covered, for 1 hour. Purée the soup in batches in a blender and strain through a fine sieve into a bowl. Stir in the cubed cucumber, heavy cream, dillweed, lemon juice, Tabasco sauce, salt and white pepper. Chill, covered, for several hours. Adjust the seasonings. Serve the soup in chilled bowls. Garnish each serving with a teaspoon of diluted sour cream and a sprinkling of chopped fresh dillweed or chives.

Ginger Carrot Soup

Yield: 6 servings

Sweet and zesty flavors combined with a smooth texture invite you to savor each sip.

3 tablespoons butter
1 cup chopped onion
3 tablespoons minced crystallized ginger, or
    2 tablespoons minced fresh ginger
2 cups chicken broth
1 pound carrots, peeled and sliced
1/2 teaspoon ground coriander
1 cup orange juice
3/4 cup milk
1/2 teaspoon salt
1/8 teaspoon white pepper
Additional milk or cream

Melt the butter in a large saucepan over medium heat. Sauté the onion and ginger in the butter until the onion is tender but not browned. Stir in the chicken broth, carrots and coriander. Simmer, covered, for 25 minutes or until the carrots are tender. Cool slightly. Purée the soup in batches in a blender. Return the soup to the saucepan and stir in the orange juice, milk, salt and white pepper. Cook until heated through, being careful not to boil. Thin with a little milk or cream if needed. Serve the soup hot or at room temperature. Garnish each serving with finely chopped parsley.

Cream of Cauliflower Soup

Yield: about 8 servings

Puréed vegetables give this soup a rich, creamy texture. You will love its ease of preparation.

1 large head cauliflower, coarsely chopped
1 large leek, white part only, coarsely
    chopped
2 potatoes, peeled and coarsely chopped
6 cups chicken broth
1/2 cup cream
2 tablespoons butter
Salt and pepper to taste

Combine the cauliflower, leek, potatoes and chicken broth in a 6-quart soup pot. Bring to a boil. Reduce the heat and simmer until the vegetables are tender. Purée in batches in a blender. Return the soup to the soup pot and stir in the cream, butter, salt and pepper. Serve hot or at room temperature. Garnish each serving with freshly ground pepper.

The Ballet of the Hats

In the early days, fashion shows were rather more formal than they are now because formality was more in vogue in society. Ladies wore elaborate, elegant hats at that time, quite large hats, in fact, that were as beautiful as the flower arrangements that graced the tables.

In order to accommodate the demand for fashion show reservations, guests were closely seated for lunch. Striking rows of hats could be seen at either side of the tables, turning left and right as conversation demanded. When the servers brought the soup or entrée, hats could be seen tilting to the right as food was presented and to the left as dishes were removed in a gentle sway that almost looked choreographed.

Gone now are the days of the hats, but the memories are vivid and lasting.

Cream of Corn Soup

Yield: 6 servings

Expect a bounce in flavor and texture with the addition of crushed tortilla chips to this upgraded version of a favorite soup served at the Restaurant since 1977.

2 tablespoons olive oil
1/4 cup finely chopped green and/or red bell peppers
1/4 cup finely chopped celery
2 tablespoons finely chopped onion
1/8 teaspoon cayenne pepper, or to taste
1/4 teaspoon black pepper
1 1/2 teaspoons salt, or to taste
2 cups chicken broth
1 1/2 cups milk
3/4 cup half-and-half
2 tablespoons canned diced green chiles (optional)
1 (15-ounce) can cream-style corn
1 cup lightly crushed tortilla chips
Additional milk or chicken broth

Heat the olive oil in a large saucepan over medium heat. Add the bell peppers, celery, onion, cayenne pepper, black pepper and salt. Reduce the heat to low and sauté the vegetables until tender, stirring frequently. Stir in the chicken broth. Add the milk, half-and-half, green chiles, corn and tortilla chips. Simmer, covered, for 20 minutes. Reduce the heat to very low and steep for 1 hour to further develop the flavors, if desired. Adjust the seasonings. Thin with milk or chicken broth, if needed. Serve the soup hot. Garnish each serving with finely chopped parsley or cilantro.

Wrought Iron Candlesticks and the Charred Hat

It was always fashionable to purchase items created by the artisans at the Guild and display them on the premises wherever possible. In the 1930s, the members bought two wrought iron candlesticks over five feet tall, created by Guild craftsman Silvestre. They were put on display in a perfect spot—on both sides of the niche by the kitchen in the dining room. A large candle was placed in each candlestick and lit every day at lunchtime. It was a lovely sight to behold.

In those days, women always wore rather elaborate hats to lunch. One day, as a patron stood beside one of the candlesticks chatting with a server, the veil on her hat began to smoke up! Unaware of her predicament, she was completely astonished when servers immediately began hitting her on the head with napkins to keep her veil from further charring.

What a catastrophe! Needless to say, that was the end of the beautiful candlesticks.

Double Mushroom Velvet Soup

Yield: 4 to 5 servings

Earthy flavors of white and wild mushrooms combined with dry sherry and sour cream lift this soup to the sublime.

1 ounce dried wild mushrooms, broken into small pieces
$^1/_2$ cup dry sherry
2 tablespoons butter
1 cup chopped onion
8 ounces button mushrooms, sliced
$^1/_2$ cup minced Italian parsley
$^1/_8$ teaspoon basil
2 tablespoons all-purpose flour
4 cups beef broth, heated
1 cup sour cream or crème fraîche

Steep the wild mushrooms in the sherry in a small bowl for 30 minutes. Drain the mushrooms, reserving the sherry. Strain the sherry through a coffee filter or paper towel. Melt the butter in a large saucepan over medium heat. Sauté the onion in the butter just until limp. Stir in the wild mushrooms, button mushrooms, parsley and basil. Cook until the vegetables are tender. Sprinkle the flour over the vegetables. Cook for 1 to 2 minutes, stirring constantly. Whisk in the reserved sherry and beef broth. Bring to a boil. Reduce the heat and simmer, covered, for 45 minutes.

Remove 2 cups of the mushrooms and broth. Process in a blender or food processor until smooth. Whisk into the sour cream in a mixing bowl. Ladle about 2 cups of the mushrooms and the liquid from the large saucepan slowly into the sour cream mixture, whisking constantly. Stir the sour cream mixture into the large saucepan just before serving. Adjust the seasonings. Serve the soup hot. Garnish each serving with chopped Italian parsley. Reheat the soup carefully without boiling.

Wild Mushrooms

Mushrooms most frequently found in dried form are boletes, French cèpes, Italian porcini, morels, black chanterelles, and shiitake. As a general rule, one ounce of dried is equivalent to one pound of fresh. To reconstitute, soak in hot water or dry sherry for fifteen to thirty minutes. Several layers of paper towels or a coffee filter set in a strainer works just fine for straining the water to remove any sand or grit. You can then use the rehydrating water as a delicious addition to soups and sauces.

Autumn Red Pepper Soup

Yield: 10 to 11 servings

Make this nutritious and flavorful soup at the end of summer when peppers are plentiful and inexpensive. Serve hot or cold.

3 tablespoons butter
2 tablespoons olive oil
6 large red, yellow or orange bell peppers or
   a mix, seeded and chopped
3 carrots, peeled and thinly sliced
1/2 small fennel bulb, sliced and chopped
   (reserve fennel leaves for garnish)
3 large shallots, chopped
1 large garlic clove, chopped
5 cups chicken broth
2 small tart green apples, peeled and chopped
1/8 teaspoon red pepper flakes, or to taste
Salt to taste
Cayenne pepper to taste (optional)
Heavy cream

Heat the butter and olive oil in a 6-quart soup pot over medium heat. Add the bell peppers, carrots, fennel, shallots and garlic. Sauté for 10 minutes or just until the vegetables are tender, stirring frequently. Stir in the chicken broth, apples and red pepper flakes. Bring to a boil. Reduce the heat and simmer, covered, for 30 minutes or until the apples and vegetables are tender. Purée the soup in batches in a blender and strain through a sieve into a large bowl. Return to the soup pot and reheat over low heat. Add the salt and cayenne pepper. Serve the soup hot, chilled or at room temperature. Top each serving with 1 teaspoon heavy cream swirled on the top and a sprinkling of chopped fennel leaves.

Mother's Day on the Terrace

Santa Fe Pumpkin Soup

Yield: 9 servings

Pungent spices coalesce to produce one of the most delicious southwestern flavors your taste buds will ever encounter. Don't wait for autumn to enjoy!

6 cups chicken broth
1 (29-ounce) can pumpkin purée, or 4 cups
   puréed fresh pumpkin
3 tablespoons dark brown sugar
2 teaspoons cumin
1 teaspoon chili powder
1 teaspoon ground coriander
1/4 teaspoon cayenne pepper
1/4 teaspoon mace
1 1/2 cups heavy cream
3 tablespoons lime juice
Salt to taste

Combine the chicken broth, pumpkin, brown sugar, cumin, chili powder, coriander, cayenne pepper and mace in a large soup pot and bring to a boil. Reduce the heat and simmer for 20 minutes or until slightly thickened, stirring occasionally. Stir in the cream. Simmer for 10 minutes, stirring occasionally. Adjust the seasonings to taste. Add the lime juice and salt just before serving. Serve hot garnished with toasted corn tortilla strips.

The Bun in the Hat Trick

Hats have certainly played a large role in the history of Allied Arts Guild Restaurant.

One time, a patron wearing a "cartwheel hat," quite large and fashionable at the time, was having lunch on the terrace. One of the servers accidentally managed to drop one of our petite rolls into the hat. The server came back to the kitchen saying, "Oh, I don't know what to do. I dropped a bun on this woman's hat and it's still in there."

Because the woman was unaware she had a bun on her hat, the server was loath to call it to the woman's attention. The kitchen staff urged her to return and remove the bun. So, she bravely walked up to the lady with the hat, graciously excused herself, reached for the bun, and remove it she did!

Tomato Basil Soup

Yield: about 8 servings

If you enjoy rich, creamy soups, but want to avoid the high calories of cream, try this full-bodied vegetable purée instead. Quick and easy to prepare, it's really a winner.

3 tablespoons butter
1 large onion, chopped
1 large carrot, peeled and shredded
4 cups chicken broth
1 (28-ounce) can crushed tomatoes
     with basil
1/4 cup packed fresh basil leaves
1/2 teaspoon sugar
1/8 teaspoon cayenne pepper
1 teaspoon salt, or to taste

Melt the butter in a 3- or 4-quart saucepan over medium heat. Sauté the onion and carrot in the butter until the onion is tender. Stir in the chicken broth, tomatoes, basil, sugar, cayenne pepper and salt. Bring to a boil, stirring constantly. Reduce the heat and simmer, covered, for 10 minutes or until the carrots are tender. Purée the soup in batches in a blender. Garnish the soup with garlic- or herb-flavored croutons and top with shaved Parmesan cheese.

Zucchini Bisque Delight

Yield: 7 servings

A popular standby at the Restaurant, this vegetable purée lives up to its name. We serve it hot in the winter and cold in the summer.

1/4 cup (1/2 stick) butter
1 cup chopped onion
2 pounds zucchini, coarsely chopped
3 1/2 cups chicken broth
1/2 cup half-and-half
1/2 teaspoon salt
1/8 teaspoon pepper
1/8 teaspoon freshly ground nutmeg
1/8 teaspoon tarragon

Heat the butter in a large saucepan over medium-low heat. Sauté the onion in the butter until tender. Add the zucchini and chicken broth. Bring to a boil. Reduce the heat and simmer until the zucchini is tender. Purée in batches in a blender. Add the half-and-half, salt, pepper, nutmeg and tarragon just before serving. Serve the soup hot or cold. Garnish each serving with freshly chopped parsley or chives.

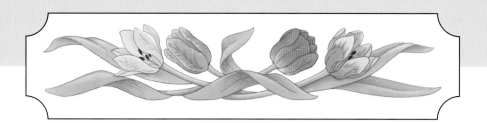

Vegetable Lentil Soup

Yield: 12 servings

The deep and complex flavors of this soup will delight the vegetarian palate. It will make a meal in itself.

3 cups water
1 cup green or brown lentils
6 cups chicken broth or vegetable broth
1 cup chopped seeded peeled tomatoes
3/4 cup peeled cubed thin-skinned potatoes (red, white or Yukon Gold)
1 onion, finely chopped
1 celery rib, cut into 1/4-inch pieces
1 carrot, peeled and cut into 1/4-inch pieces
2 garlic cloves, finely minced
1 teaspoon cumin seeds
1 teaspoon ground coriander
1/4 cup chopped cilantro
Grated zest of 1/4 lemon
Juice of 1 lemon
1 teaspoon salt, or to taste
1/3 teaspoon pepper

Bring the water to boil in a saucepan and stir in the lentils. Reduce the heat to medium-low and simmer for 15 minutes or just until the lentils are tender. Drain and set aside. Combine the chicken broth, tomatoes, potatoes, onion, celery, carrot and garlic in a large soup pot and bring to a boil. Reduce the heat and simmer for 30 minutes. Add the cumin seeds and coriander. Simmer for 15 minutes longer. Stir in the lentils, cilantro, lemon zest, lemon juice, salt and pepper just before serving. Serve the soup hot. Garnish each serving with chopped cilantro and pass slices of lemon or lime to squeeze into the soup.

The Wayward Conception

The Auxiliary's pursuit of correctness was challenged one day in the early years of post-war luncheon service.

A sweet elderly guest, noting the large number of young mothers-to-be serving lunch, commented that the lunchroom looked like an operation run by a Home for Wayward Girls!

The Auxiliary members were loath to take notice of this outspoken guest, but hear her they did!

At the next general meeting of all the volunteers, they immediately decided that all volunteers appearing in "such condition" should work behind the scenes, either in the kitchen or at the reservation desk. From then on, the lunchroom servers were never again viewed as wayward girls.

Creole Soup

Yield: 7 to 8 servings

To enjoy this soup as a main course, add slices of cooked andouille sausage and serve with hot French bread.

2 (11-ounce) cans beef consommé
3¹/₂ cups water
1 (15-ounce) can diced tomatoes
¹/₂ cup finely chopped green bell pepper
¹/₂ cup finely chopped onion
¹/₂ cup finely chopped carrots
¹/₄ teaspoon oregano
¹/₄ teaspoon pepper
1 bay leaf
¹/₂ cup uncooked shell pasta
¹/₄ teaspoon Creole seasoning, or to taste
Salt to taste

Combine the beef consommé, water, tomatoes, bell pepper, onion, carrots, oregano, pepper and bay leaf in a large soup pot. Bring to a boil. Reduce the heat and simmer, covered, for 1 hour. Add the pasta and cook until al dente. Add the Creole seasoning and salt. Remove the bay leaf. Garnish the soup with finely chopped Italian parsley.

Incorporate this vegetable base into soups, pasta, or pasta sauce for an additional boost in flavor.

Italian Vegetable Base

*Yield: 6 to 8 servings for soup,
4 to 6 servings for pasta*

Process ¹/₂ cup shredded carrots, ¹/₂ cup lightly packed, chopped Italian parsley leaves, 4 roughly chopped garlic cloves and 3 tablespoons olive oil in a blender or food processor until smooth. Pour into a jar. Drizzle top with 1 tablespoon olive oil. Cover and refrigerate.

To use, add 1 teaspoon per bowl to almost any vegetable-based soup; stir directly into cooked pasta; or add to any tomato-based sauce for a simple flavor enhancement.

Italian Market Soup

Yield: 20 servings

Reminiscent of the traditional bean soups of Tuscany, this hearty soup makes a simple but pleasing meal when combined with a green salad, Italian bread, and a glass of chianti. Make the soup ahead to allow the flavors to blend. It freezes well, too.

3 quarts water
1 (16-ounce) package 15-bean mix
1 ham bone, or 3 ham hocks
1 (28-ounce) can diced tomatoes
2 large onions, chopped
4 celery ribs, chopped
2 garlic cloves, minced
2 bay leaves
1 teaspoon dried marjoram
1 teaspoon dried thyme leaves
$^1/_2$ teaspoon dried rosemary, crumbled
1 pound mild Italian sausage, casings removed and sausage halved and sliced
$^3/_4$ cup dry red wine
1 teaspoon salt, or to taste

Combine the water, beans and ham bone in a 6-quart soup pot. Bring to a boil. Reduce the heat and simmer, covered, for 2 hours. Add the tomatoes, onions, celery, garlic, bay leaves, marjoram, thyme and rosemary. Simmer, covered, for about 1 hour. Add the sausage and simmer, covered, for 30 to 40 minutes longer. Stir in the wine and simmer for 10 minutes longer. Remove the ham bone and let cool. Remove the meat from the bones. Chop or shred the meat and return it to the soup pot. Discard the bay leaves. Chill, covered, for 8 hours. Skim off the hardened fat. Reheat the soup and stir in the salt. Garnish each serving with chopped Italian parsley and pass a bowl of grated Parmesan cheese, shredded Monterey Jack cheese or shredded manchego cheese.

Springtime Garden

Specialty Salads and Dressings

Weddings and Receptions

The spectacular garden views and the historic architecture of the Allied Arts Guild Restaurant's terrace, dining room, and Cervantes Court contribute to an unparalleled romantic atmosphere for weddings and receptions. In the spring and summer, guests can flow freely among the three rooms, taking advantage of the ever-changing visual delights—some wisteria here, a mural there.

The Auxiliary provides everything from the floral centerpiece on the lace-covered food table to the magnificent sterling silver tea service on the beverage table. The bride has only to supply her own cake and any music she and her new spouse desire.

No reasonable bridal request is refused. We do everything from accommodating very last-minute dietary restrictions to making Nana Laminski's stuffed cabbage rolls. Nana's original cabbage roll recipe involved such directions as "crush up 16 Ritz crackers and add 3 handfuls of milk." While our cooks found these directions challenging, the rolls ended up holding a place of honor on the buffet table.

Couples choose from three formats for their reception: a stand-up affair with an assortment of hors d'oeuvre, a buffet luncheon preceded by a few hors d'oeuvre, or a sit-down luncheon, also preceded by a few hors d'oeuvre. The majority of young couples choose the buffet luncheon. No one goes home hungry.

As the day progresses, tradition prevails. Toasts are given, dancing is enjoyed, the cake is cut and the bouquet is thrown. Amid the lovely setting that is the Allied Arts Guild Restaurant, another happy couple is launched on its way toward, what will hopefully become, a lifetime of happy togetherness.

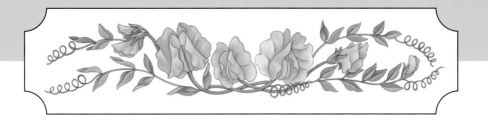

Allied Arts Guild Restaurant Presents

A Wedding Reception Buffet

Pre-Reception Appetizers

Bite-Size Crab Quiches

Spicy Surprise Puffs

Indonesian Chicken Satay

Vegetable Basket with Quick Curry Dip and Dill Dressing

White Wine and Wedding Punch

Buffet Menu

Chilled Turmeric Rice

Thai Noodle Salad

Spinach Salad Taverna with Paprika Dressing

Fresh Fruit Platter

Special Occasion Beef Tenderloin Slices with Horseradish Sauce

Cheese Tortellini Primavera

Baked Chicken Tenders with Lemon Ginger Sauce

*Assorted Melba Toast and French Bread Slices with Roasted Gilroy Garlic Dip,
Beer Cheese Balls and Liverwurst Pâté Spread*

White and Red Wines, Wedding Punch

Wedding Cake

Champagne, Coffee, Tea

Benefiting the Lucile Packard Children's Hospital at Stanford

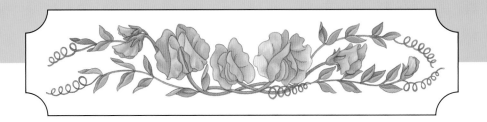

Cranberry Holiday Salad

Yield: 10 servings

Make this bright and festive salad whenever the occasion calls for something special.

Cranberry Dressing
1 cup fresh or frozen unsweetened cranberries
1 cup vegetable oil
1/2 cup Champagne vinegar or sherry vinegar
1/4 cup apple juice concentrate
1/4 cup sugar
1 teaspoon grated onion
1 teaspoon dry mustard
1 teaspoon salt

Salad
1 red apple, cubed
1 green apple, cubed
Lemon juice, orange juice or pineapple juice
1 (10-ounce) package mixed salad greens
1/2 cup dried cranberries
1/2 cup slivered almonds, toasted, or Spiced Pecans (page 33)
10 tablespoons crumbled blue cheese

For the dressing, combine the cranberries, oil, vinegar, apple juice concentrate, sugar, onion, dry mustard and salt in a blender. Process until smooth. Store any leftover dressing in the refrigerator.

For the salad, dip the apples in a little lemon juice diluted with water. Combine the apples, salad greens, dried cranberries and almonds in a large salad bowl. Drizzle the dressing over the salad just before serving and toss to combine. Arrange on individual salad plates. Top each serving with 1 tablespoon crumbled blue cheese.

Catch of the Day

One might argue that flexibility is the most important quality in a good cook and in the Auxiliary volunteers. It certainly saved the day a few years ago at the Restaurant during a wedding ceremony and reception.

The ceremony required the presence of a live goldfish, but when the goldfish was unveiled, it had died in transit. Consequently, a new fish had to be found before the ceremony could continue, and there were no pet stores that sold goldfish nearby.

The volunteers, who realized the guests would be getting restless waiting for the fish, decided to serve some of the hors d'oeuvre that were slated for the reception later in the day. They hustled to set up trays in advance while the servers passed them around in record time to the guests waiting for the fish.

Eventually the best man showed up with a lively new goldfish, and the ceremony was able to proceed. While enjoying the advanced tray of hors d'oeuvre, however, guests did not become disgruntled even though they waited more than an hour for the fisherman to return.

Italian Roasted Beet Salad

Yield: 6 to 8 servings

Shades of magenta, green, and pearly white combine to make an elegant jewel of a salad, as pleasing to the eyes as it is to the palate.

3 to 4 red beets and/or gold beets, rinsed
2 tablespoons extra-virgin olive oil
1 large bunch Italian parsley, leaves only (about 1 1/2 cups)
3 celery ribs, cut on a sharp diagonal into very thin slices
1/2 small red onion, thinly sliced into rings
2 fennel bulbs, cut into paper-thin slices (reserve leaves for garnish)
3 tablespoons extra-virgin olive oil
2 tablespoons Champagne vinegar, white wine vinegar or balsamic vinegar
Salt to taste
Freshly ground pepper to taste
2 ounces goat cheese (optional)

Grease an 8×8-inch baking pan. Preheat the oven to 350 degrees. Toss the unpeeled beets with 2 tablespoons olive oil in the prepared pan, tossing to coat well. Roast, uncovered, for 30 minutes or until the beets are tender. Let stand until cool enough to handle. Slice the beets thinly, discarding the skin, stem and root ends. Combine the parsley, celery, onion and fennel in a large bowl. Whisk 3 tablespoons olive oil and the vinegar together in a small bowl. Add the salt and pepper. Add 3/4 of the vinaigrette to the fennel mixture and toss to combine. Let stand for a few minutes. Toss the remaining vinaigrette with the beets in a mixing bowl. Arrange the beets on individual salad plates. Top with the fennel mixture. Garnish with chopped fennel leaves and crumbled goat cheese.

Note: When preparing fresh beets, wear gloves to prevent stained fingers. If your hands or cutting board becomes stained, rub salt over the stained area, and then wash with soap and water.

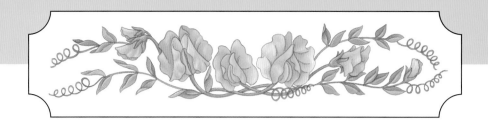

Spinach Salad Five Ways

Yield: 1 serving

Paired with our featured dressings, the following salad variations will add flavor and nutrition to any meal.

Spinach Salad Taverna
  2 to 3 cups salad-size spinach leaves, rinsed, dried and chilled
  Paprika Dressing (page 83)
  1 tablespoon marinated sun-dried tomato pieces
  2 teaspoons toasted pine nuts
  2 tablespoons crumbled feta cheese

Spinach and Mushroom Salad
  2 to 3 cups salad-size spinach leaves, rinsed, dried and chilled
  Paprika Dressing (page 83) or Confetti Dressing (page 82)
  2 small white mushrooms, thinly sliced
  2 tablespoons shredded carrots

Fruited Spinach Salad
  2 to 3 cups salad-size spinach leaves, rinsed, dried and chilled
  Honey Mustard Dressing (page 82) or Paprika Dressing (page 83)
  3 large strawberries, sliced, or apple chunks
  3 mandarin orange segments or pear chunks
  1 tablespoon crumbled blue cheese
  4 to 6 sugared pecans or Spiced Pecans (page 33)

Bacon and Egg Spinach Salad
  2 to 3 cups salad-size spinach leaves, rinsed, dried and chilled
  Confetti Dressing (page 82) or Buttermilk Dressing (page 76)
  1 slice bacon, crisp-cooked and crumbled
  $^1/_2$ hard-cooked egg, finely chopped
  1 tablespoon finely chopped green onions

Italian Spinach Salad
  2 to 3 cups salad-size spinach leaves, rinsed, dried and chilled
  Italian Salad Dressing (page 83)
  3 tomato wedges
  3 slices hard-cooked egg
  2 small white mushrooms, thinly sliced
  1 tablespoon Swiss cheese, cut into small cubes

Select one of the salad variations. Place the spinach in a bowl. Add the desired amount of dressing and toss to combine. Arrange on an individual salad plate and add the remaining ingredients from the chosen salad variation.

Sesame Chicken Salad

Yield: 15 servings

Seeds, nuts, and chow mein noodles add a pleasant crunch to the blanched green vegetables in this salad chock-full of Far Eastern flavors.

Sesame Dressing

1 cup vegetable oil
1/3 cup sesame oil
1/2 cup rice wine vinegar
3 tablespoons soy sauce
2 tablespoons sugar
1/4 teaspoon chili oil
1/2 envelope seasoning mix from chicken-flavored
   ramen noodles
1/8 teaspoon salt
1/8 teaspoon pepper

Salad

4 cups shredded cooked chicken
4 cups finely shredded cabbage
2 cups broccoli florets, blanched
2 cups snow peas, blanched and halved on the diagonal
3/4 cup coarsely chopped cashews, toasted
2 tablespoons sesame seeds, toasted
1/2 cup coarsely chopped cilantro
1/2 cup chopped green onions
1 1/2 packages chicken-flavored ramen noodles, crushed
Red leaf lettuce

For the dressing, combine the vegetable oil, sesame oil, vinegar, soy sauce, sugar, chili oil, seasoning mix, salt and pepper in a small bowl and whisk until blended.

For the salad, combine the chicken and 1/4 of the dressing in a medium bowl and mix well. Marinate, covered, in the refrigerator until serving time. Combine the cabbage, broccoli, snow peas, cashews, sesame seeds, cilantro, green onions and ramen noodles in a large bowl. Chill, covered, until serving time. Add the chicken and remaining dressing to the cabbage mixture and toss well. Adjust the seasonings. Serve on a bed of red leaf lettuce. Garnish with sprigs of cilantro.

Serve this sparkling punch for any occasion that requires a punch bowl. The orange ice ring adds extra beauty and elegance to the presentation.

Wedding Punch

1 quart lemonade concentrate
3 quarts chilled water
2 cups chilled pineapple juice
1/2 (10-ounce) package frozen sliced
   strawberries, thawed
2 tablespoons limeade concentrate
1/2 liter chilled 7-Up or Sprite
1 orange ice ring

In a large punch bowl with a greater than 6-quart capacity, combine the lemonade concentrate, water, pineapple juice, strawberries, limeade concentrate and 7-Up or Sprite. Refrigerate until ready to serve. Just before serving, gently lower the orange ice ring into the bowl with the design side facing up.

Orange Ice Ring

Place washed orange leaves, shiny side facing down, around the bottom of a round ring mold that will fit into your punch bowl. Tuck sliced orange pieces between the leaves to form a pattern. Put 2 cups ice cubes on top of orange slices. Add 1 cup cold water and freeze. Once frozen, fill mold to top with water and freeze. Unmold into punch bowl with design facing up.

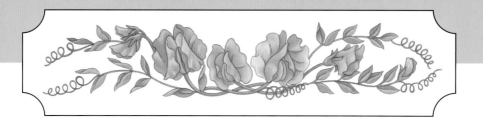

Southwest Chicken Salad

Yield: 6 servings

Make this salad in three stages and assemble at the last minute. Each component can also stand alone.

Black Bean Salsa

1 (15-ounce) can black beans, drained
  and rinsed
1 cup fresh, frozen or canned yellow corn
1 cup finely chopped celery
1/2 cup finely chopped red bell pepper
1/4 cup sliced green onions

2 teaspoons finely minced seeded jalapeño chile
2 tablespoons chopped cilantro
2/3 cup apple cider vinegar
1/3 cup vegetable oil
1 tablespoon sugar

Chili Marinade

1/4 cup vegetable oil
4 teaspoons Dijon mustard
1 tablespoon chili powder

2 teaspoons paprika
1/2 teaspoon cumin
1/4 teaspoon cayenne pepper

Buttermilk Dressing

2 cups buttermilk
1 cup mayonnaise

4 ounces feta cheese, crumbled
1/2 teaspoon cumin

Chicken and Assembly

6 chicken breasts, cut diagonally into 1-inch strips
Red leaf lettuce

For the salsa, combine the black beans, corn, celery, bell pepper, green onions, jalapeño chile and cilantro in a large bowl. Combine the vinegar, oil and sugar in a small bowl and mix well. Stir into the bean mixture. Let stand for at least 2 hours, stirring occasionally. Drain before using.

For the marinade, combine the oil, Dijon mustard, chili powder, paprika, cumin and cayenne pepper in a small bowl and mix well.

For the dressing, combine the buttermilk, mayonnaise, cheese and cumin in a small bowl and mix well.

For the chicken, coat the chicken pieces with the marinade in a shallow dish. Marinate in the refrigerator for 1 hour. Remove the chicken from the marinade and discard the marinade. Grill the chicken over medium-hot coals for 3 minutes on each side or until cooked through. Let cool. Substitute Spicy Chicken Bites, page 81, for the chicken, if desired.

To assemble, line salad plates with lettuce. Spoon 1/2 to 2/3 cup of the drained salsa onto the center of each plate. Fan the chicken strips to the side of the salsa. Top with the dressing. Garnish with avocado slices, black olives and cherry or grape tomatoes. Pass the extra dressing in a separate bowl.

Exotic Turkey Salad

Yield: 8 or 9 servings

Introduced at the Restaurant in 1981, this popular salad, laced with a distinctly pungent dressing, makes good use of leftover turkey. It requires two hours' chilling.

Ginger Curry Dressing
$1/2$ cup mayonnaise
$1/2$ cup sour cream
2 tablespoons minced crystallized ginger
1 tablespoon curry powder, or to taste
2 teaspoons soy sauce
1 teaspoon fresh lemon juice
1 teaspoon salt

Salad
$51/2$ cups cubed roasted turkey
2 (8-ounce) cans water chestnuts, drained and chopped
$11/2$ cups halved red seedless grapes
$11/3$ cups chopped celery
$1/3$ cup thinly sliced green onion tops
Chilled greens

For the dressing, combine the mayonnaise, sour cream, crystallized ginger, curry powder, soy sauce, lemon juice and salt in a small bowl and mix well. Adjust the seasonings. Chill until serving time.

For the salad, combine the turkey, water chestnuts, grapes, celery and green onions in a large bowl. Add the dressing and toss to combine. Chill for at least 2 hours. Adjust the seasonings. Serve the salad on a bed of chilled greens. Garnish the tops with toasted almonds and the sides with fresh fruit.

Wedding Cakes

When the Auxiliary first hosted weddings at the Restaurant, food service included the wedding cake as well. A beautifully frosted cake would be ordered, and members decorated the cake with gardenias and ferns. A knife decorated with lilies of the valley or gardenias was used to cut the cake.

Today's brides provide the wedding cake of their choice and often the keepsake knife themselves. Cakes are delivered well before the reception and decorated on site by the volunteers.

One wedding cake began to tilt so precipitously soon after it was delivered, à la the Leaning Tower of Pisa, that it had to be dismantled and put back together in advance of its cutting! Another, frosted with whipped cream, had to be strategically stuffed with coconut to "square" it up.

Over time, guests began to respect the creativity and ingenuity of our volunteers to hold the party together, no matter what the conditions.

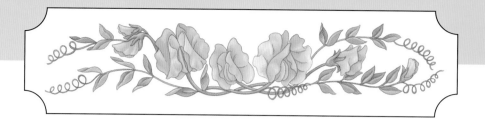

Cashew, Shrimp and Pea Salad

Yield: 6 to 8 servings

The Dill Dressing that accompanies this all-star Restaurant favorite may also be served as a sauce with fresh or cooked vegetables, as a spread for sandwiches, or as a topping for salmon.

Dill Dressing
1/3 cup mayonnaise
1/3 cup sour cream
2 tablespoons lemon juice
1 tablespoon chopped fresh dillweed
1 teaspoon salt
1/2 teaspoon lemon pepper or citrus pepper seasoning
1/8 teaspoon Oriental chili paste

Salad
1 pound peeled cooked salad shrimp, drained and dried
Juice of 1/2 lemon
3 cups frozen petite peas, thawed, drained and dried
1 cup thinly sliced celery
1/2 cup thinly sliced green onions
1/3 cup finely chopped red bell pepper
1/3 cup finely chopped yellow bell pepper
1/2 cup lightly toasted coarsely chopped cashews
Chilled greens

Wedding Celebration

For the dressing, combine the mayonnaise, sour cream, lemon juice, dillweed, salt, lemon pepper and chili paste in a small bowl and mix well. Adjust the seasonings to taste. Chill until serving time.

For the salad, combine the shrimp and lemon juice in a bowl. Chill for 10 minutes. Drain the shrimp and pat dry on paper towels. Combine the shrimp, peas, celery, green onions, bell peppers and cashews in a large bowl. Add the dressing and toss to combine. Chill, covered, until serving time. Adjust the seasonings to taste. Serve the salad on a bed of chilled greens. Garnish with thin strips of red bell pepper, yellow bell pepper and sprigs of fresh dillweed or seasonal fresh fruit.

Shrimp and Capellini Salad

Yield: 6 to 8 servings

A bride's favorite for that special wedding buffet, this salad has been served at the Restaurant since 1988.

3/4 cup mayonnaise
1/4 cup fresh lemon juice
1/2 cup grated Parmesan cheese
1 pound peeled cooked salad shrimp, drained and dried
1/4 cup fresh lemon juice
1 (10-ounce) package capellini or angel hair pasta,
   broken into thirds
1 1/2 cups minced celery
1/2 cup thinly sliced green onions
1/2 cup bottled or homemade Italian Salad dressing
   (see Italian Salad Dressing, page 83)
5 ounces frozen petite peas, thawed and drained
   (1/2 of a 10-ounce package)
Salt and pepper to taste
Chilled salad greens

Combine the mayonnaise, 1/4 cup lemon juice and the cheese in a small bowl and mix well. Chill, covered, until serving time. Combine the shrimp and 1/4 cup lemon juice in a small bowl. Marinate for about 20 minutes. Cook the capellini using the package directions; drain and rinse. Place the shrimp in a large bowl, reserving 5 for the garnish. Add the pasta, celery, green onions and salad dressing and toss to combine. Marinate in the refrigerator for 2 to 3 hours, preferably overnight.

Add the peas and mayonnaise dressing to the shrimp mixture and toss to combine. Add the salt and pepper. Serve on a platter lined with chilled salad greens. Garnish the top with the reserved shrimp and freshly chopped parsley. Add fresh vegetables, olives or marinated artichokes around the sides.

The Joy of Flowers

For many years, our talented Auxiliary volunteers created all the magnificent floral centerpieces prepared for the buffet table at wedding receptions. The members would start by ascertaining the brides' colors. They would then beg, borrow and sweet-talk flowers from members' gardens, as well as their own, to build spectacular arrangements that graced the tables. Delphiniums, foxgloves and roses all magically appeared in the bouquets. Most came from the gardens of our own members. Occasionally a few were bought.

The Auxiliary has never been shy of members who possess the skills and materials required to keep the Restaurant decorated. Lavish floral arrangements adorned the Restaurant at special events, and festive greens embellished the fireplaces during the holidays.

Retiring members have always passed the torch on to other talented volunteers. Without a doubt, the wonderful traditions that have flourished for so many years will continue to thrive with the recruitment of new members.

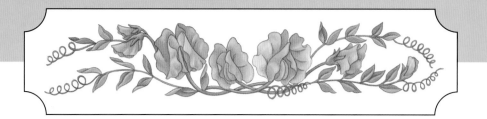

Thai Noodle Salad

Yield: 10 to 12 servings

This special-occasion salad is inspired by flavors of the Orient. It requires two days in the making but is well worth the time and effort.

Thai Dressing

3/4 cup rice wine vinegar
1/2 cup soy sauce
3 tablespoons sesame oil
2 tablespoons sugar

2 tablespoons grated fresh ginger
2 garlic cloves, minced
2 tablespoons fresh lemon juice
1/4 teaspoon chili oil

Ginger Marinade

1 cup chopped green onions
2 tablespoons chopped peeled fresh ginger
2 garlic cloves
1 cup soy sauce

1/3 cup sugar
1 tablespoon toasted sesame seeds
1 teaspoon sesame oil

Salad

11/2 pounds pork tenderloin, trimmed
8 ounces capellini, broken into thirds
1 cup bean sprouts, rinsed and drained
1 cup chopped red bell pepper
3/4 cup thinly sliced peeled English cucumber

1/2 cup chopped green onions
1/3 cup chopped fresh basil
1/3 cup chopped fresh cilantro
Salad greens

For the dressing, combine the vinegar, soy sauce, sesame oil, sugar, ginger, garlic, lemon juice and chili oil in a small bowl and mix well.

For the marinade, combine the green onions, ginger and garlic in a small food processor and process to a smooth paste. Combine with the soy sauce, sugar, sesame seeds and sesame oil in a bowl and mix well.

For the salad, place the pork tenderloin in the marinade in a shallow dish, turning to coat all sides. Marinate, covered, in the refrigerator overnight, turning at least once. Preheat the oven to 325 degrees. Remove the tenderloin from the marinade and discard the marinade. Roast in a baking pan for 45 minutes or to 160 degrees on a meat thermometer. Let stand until cool. Cut into bite-size pieces.

Cook the capellini using the package directions; drain. Toss the hot pasta with 1/2 of the dressing in a large bowl. Let stand until cool. Add the pork, bean sprouts, bell pepper, cucumber, green onions, basil, cilantro and the remaining dressing. Toss to combine. Adjust the seasonings. Chill until serving time. Serve the salad on a bed of salad greens. Garnish with dry roasted peanuts, toasted sesame seeds or toasted cashews and seasonal vegetables.

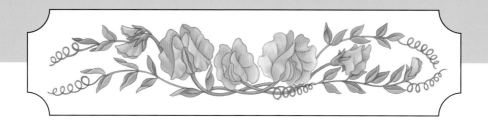

Summertime Bow Tie Pasta Salad

Yield: 8 or 9 servings

Serve this as a side salad or, during the hot days of summer, as a cold entrée. It keeps well made a day in advance.

Lemon Dijon Dressing
Juice and grated zest of 1 lemon
2 1/2 tablespoons Dijon mustard
1 teaspoon salt
1/4 teaspoon pepper
3/4 cup olive oil

Salad
12 ounces bow tie pasta
2 1/2 cups snow peas, julienned, or 1/2 cup frozen petite peas, thawed and drained
1 cup grape or cherry tomato halves (optional)
3/4 cup pine nuts, lightly toasted
3/4 cup chopped Italian parsley
3/4 pound Spicy Chicken Bites (at right), chilled

For the dressing, combine the lemon juice, lemon zest, Dijon mustard, salt and pepper in a small bowl. Whisk in the olive oil until well combined.

For the salad, cook the pasta using the package directions; drain and rinse under cold water. Combine the pasta, peas, tomatoes, pine nuts, parsley and Spicy Chicken Bites in a large bowl. Add the dressing and toss to combine. Chill, covered, until serving time. Serve the salad cold or at room temperature.

The following two methods, sautéing and baking, result in moist and flavorful chicken for tossed salads, pastas, or sandwich fillings.

Spicy Chicken Bites

Cut skinless and boneless chicken breast halves or thighs into desired size. Heat 1 tablespoon butter and 1 tablespoon olive oil in a nonstick skillet over medium high heat. Add chicken pieces, without crowding, and sprinkle tops with Creole seasoning to taste. Cook until browned on bottom, about 3 minutes. Turn chicken, sprinkle with Creole seasoning and continue cooking about 3 minutes until chicken is tender and browned. Remove from pan. Sauté remaining chicken, adding additional oil if needed.

Baked Chicken

Sprinkle chicken breast halves, including skin and bone, with salt and pepper. Place in a tightly covered baking pan. Bake in a preheated 350-degree oven 30 to 45 minutes or until chicken is tender, baked through and can easily be pulled from the bones.

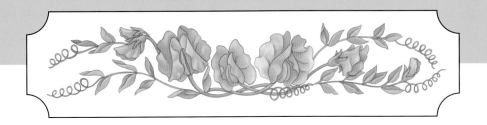

Confetti Dressing

Yield: 4 cups

Minced vegetables provide color and texture to this sweetened vinaigrette.

1 large green bell pepper, seeded and minced
1 medium white or red onion, minced
1 (4-ounce) can pimentos, drained and minced
1 cup vegetable oil
3/4 cup apple cider vinegar or tarragon vinegar
1/3 cup sugar
1 1/2 teaspoons salt

Combine the bell pepper, onion, pimentos, oil, vinegar, sugar and salt in a 1-quart jar with a tight-fitting lid and shake well. Store, tightly sealed, in the refrigerator. Shake well before serving.

Honey Mustard Dressing

Yield: 1 cup

Sweet and pungent flavors team up with poppy seeds for this favorite.

1/3 cup vegetable oil
1/3 cup fresh lemon juice
1/2 teaspoon grated lemon zest
2 tablespoons Dijon mustard
1 tablespoon honey
2 teaspoons poppy seeds

Combine the oil, lemon juice, lemon zest, Dijon mustard, honey and poppy seeds in a jar with a tight-fitting lid and shake well. Store, tightly sealed, in the refrigerator. Serve at room temperature. Shake well before serving.

The Wedding That Never Was

No wedding reception at Allied Arts was ever more memorable than the one that followed the wedding that never was.

For weeks before the planned event the bride had been having second thoughts. "Perfectly natural," proclaimed her exasperated parents. All events proceeded as planned . . . showers, luncheons, and teas. Even the rehearsal and rehearsal dinner had gone as expected on the night before the wedding.

On the morning of the wedding, however, guests arrived at the church to find a note on the door—there would be no wedding. There WOULD, however, be a reception following the non-wedding at Allied Arts Guild Restaurant, and all were welcome!

The father of the bride, having paid in full for a reception, was bound and determined that the show would go on.

Needless to say, the Auxiliary did not let him down, although a stranger or more somber reception we never did serve.

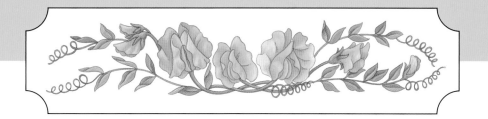

Italian Salad Dressing

Yield: 1 cup

Serve this multipurpose dressing on roasted vegetables, as well as on Italian or Greek salads.

2 tablespoons white wine vinegar
2 tablespoons fresh lemon juice
1 tablespoon Dijon mustard
1 small garlic clove, minced
$^1/_2$ teaspoon oregano
1 teaspoon salt
$^1/_4$ teaspoon freshly ground pepper
$^3/_4$ cup olive oil

Combine the vinegar, lemon juice, Dijon mustard, garlic, oregano, salt and pepper in a small bowl. Whisk in the olive oil until well combined. Pour into a jar with a tight-fitting lid. Let stand for at least 2 hours. Shake well before serving.

Paprika Dressing

Yield: 1$^1/_4$ cups

Toss this dressing on spinach salad for a perfect finish.

$^1/_4$ cup balsamic vinegar
1 tablespoon brown sugar
1 tablespoon Dijon mustard
1 tablespoon water
2 teaspoons paprika
$^1/_2$ teaspoon salt
$^1/_4$ teaspoon pepper
$^2/_3$ cup olive oil

Combine the vinegar, brown sugar, Dijon mustard, water, paprika, salt and pepper in a jar with a tight-fitting lid and shake well. Add the oil and shake until blended. Let stand until serving time. Shake well before serving. Store the unused dressing in the refrigerator for 1 week.

Original Weaver's Studio

Vegetable Variations

An American Girl Event

No event at the Allied Arts Guild Restaurant is more popular than the American Girl events. Targeting a female audience of eight to ten years in age, these shows are swamped with young ladies (and their dolls, of course), their mothers, their grandmothers, their aunties, their friends who bring their mothers, their grandmothers, their aunties and well...you get the idea. From the moment the doors open, the Restaurant vibrates with the energy that only these young ladies and their guests can generate. A second seating, equally large, follows the first.

In our first year, Samantha was the featured doll, and her party was an ice cream social. We rented tulip-shaped ice cream sundae dishes; made sauces; chopped nuts; bought sprinkles, cherries, and aerosol whipped cream; baked cookies; scooped vanilla ice cream in advance; mixed lemonade; and declared ourselves "ready." All the supplies for making sundaes, except the ice cream itself, were set on the tables. The guests were seated family style at long tables. As each table was seated, the tulip glasses filled with ice cream were brought out.

Unfortunately, chaos reigned! Mothers chatted, seemingly oblivious, while daughters were left to create their own sundaes at will. Consequently, sauce was everywhere, except on top of the ice cream. Sprinkles never made it to their intended final resting place, and aerosol whipped cream...a nightmare!

The following year, sundaes were assembled in the kitchen and delivered to the tables. "Chocolate or strawberry?" the servers would gently query. Much better! In later years, the menus, by necessity, changed. Josefina (a Hispanic doll of the Southwest) and Kit (a doll of the Great Depression) each required different menus. We always aspired to keep the menu within strict guidelines for authenticity.

Our little clients will continue to return year after year, filling our Restaurant with a sizzle of energy and delight. In future events, they can expect a changed venue to accommodate a larger and expanded audience featuring a children's fashion show, which will surely stimulate even more excitement and fun.

An American Girl Event

Hosted by The Palo Alto Auxiliary for Children, Inc.

Featuring Samantha

She is a bright, compassionate girl doll
Living with her wealthy grandmother in 1904 in a world
filled with frills and finery, parties and plays.

On Cervantes Court

Menu

*Ice Cream Sundaes topped with Chocolate and Caramel Sauces,
Whipped Cream and Nuts, Sprinkles and a Cherry*

Old Fashioned Oatmeal Cookies

Lemonade, Milk, Coffee, Tea

In the Dining Room

Film

Samantha's World

On the Terrace

Bazaar

Doll Accessories and Trinkets

Children's Books from The Linden Tree of Los Altos, CA

Announcement of Raffle Ticket Winners

Benefiting The Lucile Packard Children's Hospital at Stanford

Vegetable Medley

Yield: 4 to 6 servings

Transform everyday garden vegetables into a perfect vegetarian entrée or side dish with the addition of avocado. As an alternative, serve over rice or in taco shells.

> 1 tablespoon butter
> 1 small green bell pepper, thinly sliced
> 1 small red bell pepper, thinly sliced
> 4 small zucchini, thinly sliced
> 8 ounces mushrooms, sliced
> 2 garlic cloves, finely chopped
> 4 green onions, finely chopped
> 1 teaspoon chili powder
> 3/4 teaspoon salt, or to taste
> 2 ripe avocados, cubed

Melt the butter in a large skillet over medium heat. Add the bell peppers, zucchini, mushrooms and garlic. Sauté until the vegetables are tender crisp. Add the green onions, chili powder and salt. Fold in the avocadoes. Serve hot. Prepare the vegetables in advance, if desired. Reheat and fold in the avocados just before serving.

Dolls and Doll Houses

For several years in the 1940s, bisque dolls were raffled at the Restaurant to enhance the Auxiliary's contribution to the Hospital. These dolls were magnificently dressed in spectacular wardrobes made by our own members. Doll houses were also raffled during the Christmas season. Members decorated the houses with hand-made rugs, upholstered chairs, and petit point living room furniture.

One of the most popular doll houses was donated by Shirley Temple Black, a beloved resident of the community who gained fame not only as a child superstar, but also as a U.S. delegate to the United Nations, an ambassador to Ghana, and an ambassador to Czechoslovakia.

These popular raffles became very profitable, but were also very labor intensive. Consequently, they lasted for only a few years. The memories, however, of those golden years still linger in the minds of some of our members and will always remain a cherished segment of the Auxiliary's history.

Roasted Italian Vegetables

Yield: 6 servings

Roasting brings out the intense flavor of each and every vegetable in this beautiful presentation. Serve as a side dish or on the antipasto platter.

1 zucchini, halved lengthwise and each half cut into 3 pieces
1 red bell pepper, seeded and cut lengthwise into 1-inch strips
1 yellow or orange bell pepper, seeded and cut lengthwise into 1-inch strips
1 red onion, cut into 6 wedges
8 ounces whole mushrooms
1 thin eggplant, cut into 1/2-inch slices
1 fennel bulb, trimmed, sliced in half and layers separated
3 large garlic cloves, crushed
1/4 cup olive oil
1 teaspoon Italian seasoning
1 1/2 teaspoons salt
1/2 teaspoon pepper
2 tablespoons balsamic vinegar

Grease 2 large baking sheets. Preheat the oven to 425 degrees. Combine the zucchini, bell peppers, onion, mushrooms, eggplant, fennel and garlic in a large bowl. Combine the olive oil, Italian seasoning, salt and pepper in a small bowl and mix well. Pour over the vegetables and toss to coat. Spread the vegetables in a single layer on the prepared baking sheets. Roast for a total of about 35 minutes or until tender and browned, stirring every 10 minutes. Toss the vegetables with the vinegar. Adjust the seasonings. Garnish with torn fresh basil leaves.

Girls and Dolls

Roasted Asparagus

Yield: 4 servings

Accentuate the flavor! Roast your asparagus just once and you will never steam them again.

> 1 pound medium-thick asparagus spears,
>   tough ends removed or peeled
> 1 tablespoon olive oil
> 1 teaspoon salt
> 1/4 teaspoon pepper
> 1 lemon, cut into 6 wedges
> 2 tablespoons grated Parmesan cheese

Grease a baking sheet. Preheat the oven to 400 degrees. Combine the asparagus with the olive oil, salt and pepper on the prepared baking sheet and toss to coat the asparagus. Arrange in a single layer. Roast for 8 to 10 minutes or until fork-tender, turning the spears occasionally to prevent burning. Remove to a serving platter. Squeeze the juice of 1 or 2 lemon wedges over the asparagus. Sprinkle with the cheese. Serve hot with the remaining lemon wedges.

Sesame Green Beans

Yield: 4 servings

Sesame oil complements the flavor of the beans in this easy stove-top preparation.

> 1/2 pound green beans, stem ends removed
> 2 tablespoons butter
> 1/2 teaspoon full-flavored sesame oil
> 2 teaspoons lightly toasted sesame seeds
> Salt to taste

Plunge the beans into boiling salted water to cover in a saucepan. Cook just until tender; drain. Plunge the beans into ice water to stop the cooking; drain again. Heat the butter and sesame oil in a medium skillet until the butter melts. Add the beans and stir well. Cook until the beans are heated through, stirring constantly. Sprinkle with the sesame seeds and salt. Serve immediately.

Keeping Vegetables Green

Prolonged heat or acid quickly causes green vegetables to lose their bright color. To retain color, cook green vegetables quickly (no more than six minutes) in an uncovered pot filled with rapidly boiling, salted water until just tender.

As an alternative, microwave or stir-fry. If not serving immediately, plunge vegetables into an ice water bath in order to stop the cooking process.

Do not dress vegetables with a sauce that contains acid, such as lemon juice, tomato juice, or vinegar, until just before serving, as the acid will also dull the color.

Broccoli Casserole

Yield: 6 servings

This richly flavored vegetable dish features a creamy sauce and crunchy bread topping.

1 1/2 pounds broccoli, trimmed, or
  1 (10-ounce) package frozen chopped
  broccoli, cooked using the package
  directions
1 (10-ounce) can condensed cream
  of chicken soup
1 tablespoon all-purpose flour
1/2 cup sour cream
1/3 cup grated carrots
1 tablespoon grated onion
1/4 teaspoon salt
1/8 teaspoon pepper
3/4 cup herb-seasoned stuffing mix
1/4 cup grated Parmesan cheese
3 tablespoons butter, melted
1 teaspoon paprika

Grease a 2-quart casserole. Preheat the oven to 350 degrees. Separate the broccoli stalks from the florets. Peel the stalks and cut into 1-inch pieces. Cook the stalk pieces in boiling salted water to cover in a saucepan for 2 minutes. Add the florets. Cook for 2 to 3 minutes or just until tender; drain. Blend the soup and flour together in a large bowl. Add the sour cream, carrots, onion, salt and pepper and mix well. Stir in the broccoli. Pour into the prepared casserole. Combine the stuffing mix, cheese, butter and paprika in a small bowl and mix until crumbly. Sprinkle around the edge of the casserole. Bake for 30 to 35 minutes or until heated through and bubbly.

Cauliflower Crown

Yield: 4 to 6 servings

Do not add salt to the cooking water of cauliflower, as it will discolor the snowy white beauty of this outstanding presentation.

1 large head cauliflower, cored and leaves
  removed
Salt to taste
1/2 cup (1 stick) butter, melted
1 cup grated Parmesan cheese

Place the cauliflower in a small amount of boiling water in a large pot or in a steamer, core facing down. Cook, covered, for 25 to 30 minutes or until tender. (Or microwave, covered, on High for 6 to 9 minutes. Let stand for 3 to 4 minutes.) Preheat the broiler. Place the cauliflower head in an ovenproof serving dish, crown facing up. Sprinkle with salt. Pour the butter evenly over the top. Sprinkle with the cheese. Broil until the cheese is golden brown. Serve hot.

Carrots Zipped Up

Yield: 6 servings

Horseradish is the secret ingredient that sparks up the flavor of this easy-to-make casserole.

6 to 8 carrots, peeled and sliced on
    the diagonal
$1/2$ cup mayonnaise
2 tablespoons grated onion
1 tablespoon creamy horseradish
$1/2$ teaspoon salt
$1/4$ teaspoon pepper
$1/4$ cup dry bread crumbs
2 tablespoons butter, melted
$3/4$ teaspoon paprika

Butter a 1-quart casserole. Preheat the oven to 350 degrees. Cook the carrots in boiling salted water to cover in a saucepan just until tender; drain, reserving $1/4$ cup of the cooking water. Combine the cooking water, mayonnaise, onion, horseradish, salt and pepper in a bowl and mix well. Stir into the carrots. Pour into the prepared casserole. Combine the bread crumbs and melted butter in a small bowl and sprinkle over the carrot mixture. Sprinkle with the paprika. Bake for 15 to 20 minutes.

Copper Pennies

Yield: 6 to 8 servings

Here is another old-fashioned favorite introduced at the Restaurant decades ago. It will keep in the refrigerator for up to two weeks.

1 (10-ounce) can tomato soup
$3/4$ cup wine vinegar
Scant $2/3$ cup sugar
$1/2$ cup vegetable oil
2 teaspoons Dijon mustard
1 teaspoon Worcestershire sauce
$1/2$ teaspoon salt
2 pounds carrots, peeled and thinly sliced
    into $1/4$-inch rounds
1 green bell pepper, seeded and cut into
    small strips
1 onion, thinly sliced

Whisk the soup, vinegar, sugar, oil, Dijon mustard, Worcestershire sauce and salt together in a large bowl. Cook the carrots in boiling salted water to cover in a saucepan until tender crisp; drain. Add the carrots, bell pepper and onion to the soup mixture and toss well to coat. Marinate, covered, in the refrigerator for 12 to 24 hours, stirring occasionally. Drain well before serving. Serve cold.

Kale Kaper

Yield: 4 servings

This versatile, bold-flavored green may be served hot as a vegetable side dish or as a topping over pasta. It may also be served cold as part of an antipasto platter.

2 bunches kale
2 tablespoons olive oil
2 garlic cloves, thinly sliced
Salt to taste
1 to 2 tablespoons red wine vinegar

Strip the leaves from the kale stems. Chop the leaves and stems coarsely. Rinse under cold water; drain. Heat the olive oil in a large skillet over medium heat. Add the kale in batches, adding more kale as each batch begins to wilt, turning after each addition. Add the garlic and salt. Cook, covered, for 2 to 5 minutes. Remove the skillet from the heat and stir in the vinegar. Add more salt if needed.

Leeks in Saffron Cream Sauce

Yield: 6 servings

Unique and delicious! With saffron, the lowly leek will become a star attraction, even when served at the most formal of dinner parties.

3 large leeks, trimmed
1/4 cup heavy cream
1 pinch of saffron threads
1/2 cup heavy cream
1/2 cup freshly grated Parmesan cheese
Salt to taste

Cut the leeks in half lengthwise. Open the leaves and rinse thoroughly under cold water. Cook the leeks in boiling water in a large saucepan until tender crisp at the root ends; drain. Cut the leeks in half and return to the pan. Heat 1/4 cup heavy cream in a small saucepan over very low heat. Stir in the saffron threads and let stand for 5 minutes. Stir in 1/2 cup heavy cream and the cheese. Heat the sauce and add the salt. Spoon over the leeks. Simmer, uncovered, for 5 minutes or until the leeks are tender.

Peas and Pearls

Yield: 4 to 6 servings

We have given a French twist to an old standard. This is delicious with meat dishes but delicate enough to serve with fish.

1 cup water
2 tablespoons olive oil
1 tablespoon sugar
1/2 teaspoon herbes de Provence or fresh thyme
1 teaspoon salt, or to taste
1/4 teaspoon freshly ground pepper
1 head Boston lettuce, rinsed and cut into 2-inch strips
1 (16-ounce) package frozen petite peas and onions
1 teaspoon potato starch (optional)
1 tablespoon cold water (optional)

Combine the water, olive oil, sugar, herbes de Provence, salt and pepper in a saucepan and bring to a boil. Reduce the heat and simmer, covered, for 5 minutes. Add the lettuce. Cook, covered, for 3 minutes or until the lettuce is wilted. Let stand until serving time. Stir in the peas and onions. Cook for 3 minutes. Dissolve the potato starch in the cold water and stir into the pea mixture. Cook until the juices thicken, stirring constantly. Serve immediately.

Corn-Stuffed Tomatoes

Yield: 6 servings

This vegetable combination can be served hot with a dinner entrée or cold as a luncheon salad. Either way, the flavors will enhance any meal.

6 large firm ripe tomatoes
1 (14-ounce) can whole kernel corn, drained and patted dry
1/2 cup finely chopped red bell pepper
1/3 cup finely chopped fresh chives
1 tablespoon chopped fresh dillweed
1 teaspoon sugar
1/2 teaspoon coarsely ground pepper
1/4 teaspoon salt
2 tablespoons mayonnaise
6 tablespoons shredded Cheddar cheese

Preheat the oven to 400 degrees. Cut the tomatoes in half horizontally and scoop out the seeds. Drain the shells upside down on paper towels. Combine the corn, bell pepper, chives, dillweed, sugar, pepper and salt in a bowl and mix well. Stir in the mayonnaise. Stuff into the tomato halves and sprinkle 1 tablespoon of the cheese over each. Bake for 15 minutes. Omit the baking step, chill and serve as a cold luncheon salad, if desired.

Palate-Pleasing Potatoes

Yield: 6 servings

Parsley and garlic lend aroma and flavor to this outstanding casserole. Double or triple the recipe for a crowd.

 1/2 cup chopped fresh parsley
 4 small garlic cloves, finely chopped
 1 tablespoon extra-virgin olive oil
 1 tablespoon salt
 1 teaspoon freshly ground pepper
 3 or 4 Roma tomatoes, sliced 1/4 inch thick
 3 or 4 large russet or Yukon Gold potatoes,
  peeled and sliced 1/4 inch thick
 1/4 cup extra-virgin olive oil
 1 teaspoon paprika

Fresco of Pottery Crafts

Grease a 9×13-inch baking dish. Preheat the oven to 375 degrees. Combine the parsley, garlic, 1 tablespoon olive oil, salt and pepper in a small bowl and mix well. Spread 1/4 of the parsley mixture in the prepared baking dish. Layer 1/2 of the tomatoes, 1/2 of the potatoes and 1/2 of the remaining parsley mixture over the top. Repeat the layers. Drizzle 1/4 cup olive oil over the top. Sprinkle with the paprika. Bake, covered with foil, for 45 minutes. Remove the foil. Bake for 10 minutes longer or until the potatoes are fork-tender. Let stand for 10 minutes before serving.

Note: After peeling, Yukon Gold potatoes will not darken as quickly as other potatoes and, when cooked, will stay firmer and hold their shape longer.

Louisiana Sweet Potato Bake

Yield: 10 to 12 servings

Mashed sweet potatoes covered with a pecan streusel topping pair perfectly with turkey, chicken, ham, or pork entrées. Assemble the dish ahead and refrigerate or freeze.

> 3 1/2 pounds dark-skinned sweet potatoes
> 1/3 cup butter, melted
> 1/2 teaspoon salt, or to taste
> 1/2 teaspoon mace
> 3/4 cup milk or half-and-half
> 2 cups chopped pecans
> 1 cup packed brown sugar
> 6 tablespoons all-purpose flour
> 6 tablespoons butter, melted

Grease a 9×13-inch baking pan. Preheat the oven to 350 degrees. Bake the sweet potatoes in their jackets for 1 hour or until they are tender and caramelized inside. Scrape the pulp from the skins into a large bowl. Beat in 1/3 cup butter, the salt, mace and enough of the milk to reach a creamy consistency. Adjust the seasonings. Spread the sweet potatoes in the prepared baking pan. Combine the pecans, brown sugar, flour and 6 tablespoons butter in a bowl and mix until crumbly. Sprinkle over the sweet potatoes. Bake for 45 minutes or until hot, covering with foil partway through the cooking if the pecans are browning too rapidly. Serve hot.

The Membership Tea

Every autumn the Membership Committee sponsors a Membership Tea for the entire Auxiliary membership. The Tea honors new members and longtime members for years of service. Sometimes the Tea is held at the Restaurant, sometimes at an outside facility or even at a member's home. It is usually catered and, therefore, members come as guests—a delightful change of pace.

Provisional members often sport lovely corsages. Twenty-year members receive gold medallions. Twenty-five year members are honored with a donation to the Hospital in their name. Thirty, thirty-five, even forty-year members receive special recognition at this festive event. And yes, every year the awards are bestowed on longtime veterans, some with as many as forty to fifty years of service.

Few organizations can boast of the "staying power" of this Auxiliary, with its loyalty to the Lucile Packard Children's Hospital.

Spinach and Artichoke Casserole

Yield: 6 servings

Two vegetables team up for a flavorful duet. This is quick and easy to prepare.

1 (14-ounce) can artichoke hearts, drained
   and quartered
2 tablespoons butter
1 garlic clove, minced
1/2 cup finely chopped onion
2 (10-ounce) packages frozen creamed
   spinach, thawed
2 tablespoons mayonnaise
2 tablespoons sour cream
1/4 teaspoon salt
1/8 teaspoon Tabasco sauce, or to taste
1/3 cup freshly grated Parmesan cheese
1/2 cup fresh bread crumbs
2 tablespoons butter, melted

Grease a 1-quart casserole. Preheat the oven to 350 degrees. Place the artichokes in the prepared casserole. Melt 2 tablespoons butter in a skillet over medium heat. Add the garlic and onion and sauté for 1 minute or until translucent. Combine the onion mixture, creamed spinach, mayonnaise, sour cream, salt and Tabasco sauce in a large bowl and mix well. Adjust the seasonings. Pour over the artichokes. Combine the cheese, bread crumbs and melted butter in a small bowl and mix until crumbly. Sprinkle over the spinach mixture. Bake for 25 minutes or until lightly browned and heated through.

Spinach and Leek Bake

Yield: 8 servings

Even finicky kids will enjoy their vegetables in this unique and flavorful corn bread—and so will your sophisticated guests. The bread will keep for up to one week in the refrigerator, and it reheats beautifully.

2 leeks
1 (10-ounce) package frozen chopped
   spinach, thawed and squeezed dry
2 eggs, beaten
1 cup sour cream
1/2 cup (1 stick) butter, melted
1/4 teaspoon salt
1 (8-ounce) package corn bread muffin mix
Coarsely ground pepper to taste

Grease a 9×9-inch baking pan. Preheat the oven to 350 degrees. Cut each leek into a 9-inch length of white and green. Slice lengthwise and rinse thoroughly under cold water; drain and slice into 1-inch pieces. Combine the leeks and spinach in a food processor. Pulse until the vegetables are finely chopped. Remove to a large mixing bowl. Beat in the eggs, sour cream, butter and salt. Fold in the corn bread muffin mix. Pour into the prepared baking pan. Sprinkle pepper over the top. Bake for 25 to 30 minutes or until the center is set. Garnish the top with 1/4 cup toasted slivered almonds. Serve hot.

Ginger Zucchini Boats

Yield: 4 servings

Almonds add an unusual flavor boost and a crunchy texture to this perennial favorite. It may be assembled ahead of time.

4 medium zucchini, or 2 very large zucchini
1 tablespoon salt
2 tablespoons olive oil
1 large onion, chopped
2 carrots, shredded
1 garlic clove, minced
2 teaspoons grated fresh ginger
2/3 cup toasted slivered almonds, chopped
Salt and pepper to taste

Grease a 9×13-inch baking pan. Preheat the oven to 375 degrees. Slice the zucchini in half lengthwise. Scoop out the center of each zucchini half to make a cavity, reserving the scooped-out zucchini. Fill a 6-quart pot with water and bring to a boil. Add the salt and the zucchini. Blanch for about 3 minutes; drain. Heat the olive oil in a skillet over medium-low heat. Add the onion and sauté until translucent. Chop the reserved scooped-out zucchini and add with the carrots, garlic and ginger to the onions. Cook, covered, for 8 to 10 minutes or just until tender. Remove from the heat and stir in the almonds. Add salt and pepper. Spoon the vegetables into the zucchini halves. Place the halves in the prepared baking pan. Prepare ahead to this point and chill until baking time. Bake, covered with foil, for 15 to 20 minutes or until the zucchini are tender and heated through. Serve hot as a side dish or as a vegetarian entrée.

No More Tears

Onions release a sulfuric compound when chopped. This compound reacts with the saline in your eyes and causes them to tear. If you do not want to tear up and ruin your eye makeup, try one of the following tips recommended by our volunteers:

Chill the onions for an hour before intended use to slow down release of the sulfuric compound.

Light a candle near your work area. Or, if all else fails, grab a pair of safety glasses from the workshop and wear them.

Sweet-and-Sour Zucchini

Yield: 16 servings

Introduced at the Restaurant decades ago, the following vegetable dish, marinated in a sweet-and-sour sauce and served cold, will perk up any meal or complement any sandwich. This requires twelve to twenty-four hours marinating time before serving.

3/4 cup sugar
2/3 cup apple cider vinegar
1/2 cup white wine vinegar
1/3 cup vegetable oil
1 teaspoon dried onion flakes
1 teaspoon salt
1 teaspoon pepper
1 tablespoon chopped fresh dillweed, or 1 teaspoon dried
    dillweed (optional)
8 cups thinly sliced small zucchini (about 2 1/2 pounds)
1/2 cup finely chopped green, red, orange or yellow bell
    pepper, or a mix
1/2 cup finely chopped celery
Lettuce

Combine the sugar, apple cider vinegar, white wine vinegar, oil, onion flakes, salt, pepper and dillweed in a bowl and stir until well blended. Add the zucchini, bell peppers and celery. Marinate, covered, in the refrigerator for 12 to 24 hours, stirring occasionally. Drain well before serving. Serve on a bed of lettuce.

The Vintage Girls

Many Auxiliary members are, for whatever reason, unable to continue as active volunteers. However, they maintain their membership as "Associates," often for many, many years.

Vintage Girls are members, actively working or not, who have served the Palo Alto Auxiliary for fifteen or more years. They hold a festive luncheon in the spring where all the eligible members—both active and associate—can assemble, swap battle stories, catch up on the news, or simply renew old friendships. A good time is always had by all.

Vintage Girls are not necessarily old, nor do they wear vintage clothing, as one member thought upon receipt of her first invitation. She was actually going to look for vintage clothes at Goodwill to wear at the next meeting!

Wisteria Arbor, Artisan Studios

Exemplary Extras

Monday Morning Bridge

Over the years, the Auxiliary members developed a variety of strategies to "plump up" business on Mondays. Fashion shows, flower arranging, and package wrapping demonstrations were all successful, but not long lasting.

Suddenly, a flash of inspiration gave birth to Monday Morning Bridge. For a mere $4.00 more per person, social and duplicate bridge players could enjoy their favorite game in the serene setting of the Guild gardens, followed by their midday meal.

When the ladies arrive at 10:00 A.M. sharp, they are escorted to the terrace, where tables, chairs, cards, tallies, coffee, and tea await their friendly games. Then, when the clock strikes 12, they are moved to a different area for lunch. This practice occasioned some dismay on the part of one April guest who had been facing the terrace window at the wisteria. She was happy to become "dummy" as often as possible so she could simply turn her brain "off" and admire the spectacular view that is the Allied Arts wisteria in the spring. She did not want to give up this seat for lunch! Fortunately, her new seat in the lovely setting of Cervantes Court, the patio, more than made up for the wisteria view to which she would return after lunch.

Whether playing "social" bridge or the more hard-core "duplicate" bridge, luncheon is always a chance to relax and socialize. Hostesses, very wisely, set up the luncheon tables so that duplicate players, sometimes as many as sixteen, all eat at one large table. They really appreciate this and often comment on how refreshed they feel after their three-course luncheon—part food, part congeniality.

Many card players are delighted to take advantage of this unique opportunity. No more hosting in the confines of their own homes. Just leave all the work to us! Add to that the spectacular Allied Arts Guild setting, the contribution you are making to the Hospital, and it just doesn't get any better than that.

Monday Morning Bridge and Luncheon
At Allied Arts Guild Restaurant

On the Terrace
Enjoy Social or Duplicate Bridge with Coffee or Tea

On Cervantes Court

Choice of Hot Lunch

Gazpacho

Quiche Olé

Vegetable Medley

Salad of Mixed Greens with Pear Tomatoes and Confetti Dressing

Signature Rolls and Butter

Lemon Lovers' Delight

Coffee, Tea, Lemonade

Or Cold Lunch

Gazpacho

Capellini Salad with Shrimp

Signature Rolls and Butter

Lemon Lovers' Delight

Coffee, Tea, Lemonade

On the Terrace
Return to your game of Social or Duplicate Bridge

Benefiting the Lucile Packard Children's Hospital at Stanford

Basic Baked Rice with Four Variations

Yield: 4 to 5 servings

One of the world's most versatile side dishes can be dressed up in a variety of ways to complement any meal and celebrate any occasion.

> 1 cup long grain white rice
> 2 cups boiling chicken broth or water
> 2 tablespoons butter
> 1 teaspoon salt

Grease a 3-quart baking dish with a cover. Preheat the oven to 350 degrees. Select 1 of the 6 variations listed below. Combine the rice, chicken broth, butter, salt and before-baking ingredients in the prepared baking dish. Stir until the butter is melted. Bake, tightly covered, for 50 minutes or until the liquid has been absorbed. Fluff the rice with a fork. Stir in the after-baking ingredients. Garnish as desired.

Cranberry Rice

Before baking:
> 1/4 cup dried cranberries

After baking:
> 1/3 cup chopped toasted pecans or almonds

Lemon Dill Rice

After baking:
> 2 teaspoons dried dillweed
> 1 tablespoon grated lemon zest

Ginger Rice

Before baking:
> 2 small garlic cloves, minced
> 1 (3/4-inch) piece fresh ginger, peeled, cut in half and crushed
> 1 teaspoon lime juice
> 1/4 teaspoon turmeric

After baking:
> 1/4 cup finely chopped fresh parsley

Discard the ginger pieces.

Southwest Green Rice

Before baking:
> 4 green onions, white parts only, finely chopped (reserve the green tops)
> 1 jalapeño chile, seeded and finely chopped
> 2 tablespoons olive oil
> 1 tablespoon dry sherry

After baking:
> 1/4 cup chopped fresh parsley
> 1/4 cup finely chopped cilantro
> Reserved green onion tops, chopped

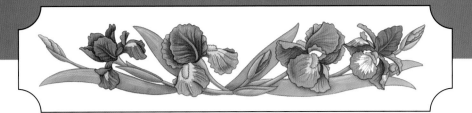

Wild Rice Vegetable Pilaf

Yield: 4 to 5 servings

Wild and long grain rice team up to produce a blend of earthy and refined flavors that no one can resist. This colorful dish will highlight any meal.

1/4 cup wild rice, rinsed
1 cup cold water
1 cup long grain white rice
2 cups boiling chicken broth or water
2 tablespoons butter
1 teaspoon salt
1/3 cup minced onion
1/3 cup minced celery
1/3 cup minced carrots

Grease a 3-quart baking dish. Preheat the oven to 350 degrees. Bring the wild rice and water to a boil in a small saucepan. Boil for 5 to 10 minutes or until the rice softens. Remove from the heat. Let stand, covered. Combine the white rice, chicken broth, butter and salt in the prepared baking pan, stirring until the butter melts. Add the onion, celery, carrots and wild rice, including any unabsorbed liquid; mix well. Bake, tightly covered, for 50 minutes. Fluff the rice with a fork. Bake, tightly covered, for 10 minutes longer or until the rice is tender and the liquid is totally absorbed. Turn off the heat and let the rice stand in the oven for 10 to 15 minutes. Fluff the rice again before serving. Garnish as desired.

Trial and Error

There was a time when the three daily courses served at Allied Arts Guild Restaurant were prepared by members or their own cooks in their homes and brought to the Restaurant. One member might whip up the soup, another the main entrée, and another the dessert. Each member would prepare a dish that she loved. Unfortunately, all the members loved rich and creamy foods.

As one past president fondly remembers, "The first time I ate lunch at the Guild, we had cream soup, a creamy main entrée, and piles of whipped cream on the dessert. Each course was wonderful, but please, hold the cream!"

Soon thereafter, a menu planning committee was established to test new recipes and determine the daily menus. As a result, meals became balanced, with particular attention paid to variety and presentation. We still love rich and creamy food, but we now adhere to our new motto: Variety is the spice of life.

Chilled Turmeric Rice

Yield: 9 to 10 servings

Turmeric gives a bright yellow color and a flavor enhancement to this side dish that is great with any meal. It's best made a day in advance.

2 cups rice
4 cups boiling vegetable broth or chicken
  broth
1 tablespoon butter
1 teaspoon turmeric
2 (6-ounce) jars marinated artichoke hearts
$1/2$ cup sliced black olives, drained
$1/4$ cup finely chopped green bell pepper
$1/4$ cup finely chopped red bell pepper
$1/2$ cup chopped green onions
$1/2$ to $3/4$ cup mayonnaise
Salt and pepper to taste
Lettuce

Lightly grease a 3-quart baking dish. Preheat the oven to 350 degrees. Combine the rice, vegetable broth, butter and turmeric in the prepared baking dish and stir until the butter melts. Bake, covered tightly with foil, for 1 hour or until the rice is tender and the liquid has been absorbed. Drain the artichoke hearts, reserving the marinade. Cut the artichoke hearts into bite-size pieces. Toss the warm rice with enough of the reserved artichoke marinade to lightly coat the rice. Chill for 1 to 8 hours. Stir in the artichoke hearts, olives, bell peppers, green onions and enough mayonnaise to moisten the salad. Add the salt and pepper. Chill thoroughly, tightly covered. Serve the rice on a bed of lettuce. Garnish the top with chopped fresh parsley and the sides with tomato wedges and other seasonal fresh vegetables.

View from the Terrace

Seasoned Orzo

Yield: 8 servings

A quickly prepared pasta side dish serves as a welcome substitute for rice and potatoes.

2 quarts water
2 tablespoons chicken base (or replace water and chicken base with 2 quarts chicken stock)
8 ounces orzo
$1/2$ tablespoon olive oil
$1/2$ tablespoon minced garlic
1 tablespoon grated lemon zest
1 tablespoon finely chopped Italian parsley
$1/4$ teaspoon pepper
Salt to taste

Bring the water to a boil in a large saucepan. Add the chicken base and stir to dissolve. Stir in the orzo. Cook for 8 minutes or until the orzo is al dente; drain and return the orzo to the saucepan. Heat the olive oil in a small saucepan over low heat. Add the garlic and sauté until tender but not browned. Add the garlic, lemon zest, parsley, pepper and salt to the orzo and mix well. Serve warm or at room temperature.

Bulgur with Garden Vegetables

Yield: about 6 servings

This appealing blend of grains and fresh vegetables serves equally well as a side dish with a meat entrée or as a salad. It's great for picnics or tailgating.

$1^1/4$ cups water
1 cup bulgur
$1/2$ teaspoon salt
1 red bell pepper, cut into $1/4$- to $1/3$-inch pieces
1 zucchini, cut into $1/4$- to $1/3$-inch pieces
1 yellow squash, cut into $1/4$- to $1/3$-inch pieces
$1/4$ red onion, coarsely chopped
$1/3$ cup toasted pine nuts
$1/4$ cup olive oil
Juice of 1 lime
$1/4$ cup minced fresh dillweed, or 4 teaspoons dried dillweed
$1/2$ teaspoon salt
$1/4$ teaspoon pepper

Bring the water to a boil in a small saucepan. Stir in the bulgur and $1/2$ teaspoon salt. Boil for 1 minute. Remove from the heat. Let stand, covered, for 15 minutes. Pour the bulgur into a large salad bowl and let cool. Stir in the bell pepper, zucchini, yellow squash, onion and pine nuts. Whisk the olive oil, lime juice, dillweed, $1/2$ teaspoon salt and pepper together in a small bowl. Pour over the salad and toss to combine. Serve cold or at room temperature.

Orange Pecan Couscous

Yield: 9 to 10 servings

Poetry Run Amok

At the annual meetings in January, outgoing officers and committee chairmen of the Palo Alto Auxiliary were expected to recite original poems before the entire general membership as their final duty in office!

This responsibility was a joy for some and a nightmare for others, depending on their skill at writing and delivering couplets, limericks, or free verse. It came naturally to the chairman of the tote bag committee, when she delighted everyone by singing her farewell poem, "Tote Bags…Tote Bags" to the tune of "A Bicycle Built for Two."

Many members, however, were so averse to writing poems that some actually stopped taking Board and Chair jobs altogether. Others accepted jobs, but hired a talented ghost member to write their poems for them.

By the end of the 1990s, outgoing officers and committee chairmen, by tacit agreement, were no longer required to write couplets, limericks, or free verse for their departures. But all the veteran members who were so joyfully entertained by the poems, while they lasted, will always treasure the fond memories.

No one can resist this refreshing, yet subtle, combination of citrus flavors that become even better after chilling overnight. Try this unique accompaniment with grilled chicken or pork.

2 cups chicken broth or vegetable broth
2 tablespoons butter
1 1/2 cups couscous
1 teaspoon salt
1/2 teaspoon pepper
1/2 cup olive oil
1/2 cup freshly squeezed orange juice
1/4 cup freshly squeezed lemon juice
1 teaspoon sugar
1 tablespoon grated orange zest
1 cup chopped toasted pecans
2/3 cup chopped green onions
1/2 cup currants
1/2 cup finely chopped Italian parsley
1 (14-ounce) can mandarin orange segments, drained, or
    2 cups fresh orange segments or halved seedless red grapes

Bring the chicken broth and butter to a boil in a large saucepan. Stir in the couscous. Remove from the heat and let stand, covered, for 5 minutes. Fluff the couscous gently with a fork. Add the salt and pepper. Let stand until cool. Whisk the olive oil, orange juice, lemon juice, sugar and orange zest together in a small bowl. Toss with the couscous, pecans, green onions, currants and parsley in a salad bowl. Stir the orange segments gently into the salad. Serve cold or at room temperature.

Golden Apricot Mold

Yield: 6 servings

During the 1970s and 1980s, gelatin molds became so popular they accompanied almost every entrée at the Restaurant. This longtime survivor possesses great color and a spicy, sparkling taste.

> 1 (15-ounce) can peeled apricot halves in
>   heavy syrup
> 1/4 cup apple cider vinegar
> 1 (3-ounce) package orange gelatin
> 1/4 teaspoon ground cloves
> 1/4 teaspoon cinnamon

Drain the apricot halves, reserving the syrup. Chop the apricots into bite-size pieces. Pour the apricot syrup into a 2-cup measure and add the vinegar and enough water to measure 2 cups liquid. Pour 1 cup of the syrup mixture into a small saucepan and bring to a boil. Remove from the heat and add the gelatin, cloves and cinnamon, stirring until the gelatin is dissolved. Stir in the remaining 1 cup syrup mixture. Chill until partially set. Fold in the apricots. Pour into a 6-cup mold or 6 individual molds. Chill until firm.

Port Wine Mold

Yield: 6 servings

Another favorite gelatin dish that has survived the test of time is this ruby-red mold. It's great served with roasted chicken, turkey, or pork.

> 1 (16-ounce) can pear halves in syrup
> 1 (3-ounce) package raspberry gelatin
> 1/2 cup port
> 2 tablespoons fresh lemon juice
> 1 (10-ounce) package frozen sweetened
>   raspberries, thawed but not drained

Drain the pears, reserving the syrup. Chop the pears into bite-size pieces. Pour the pear syrup into a 1-cup measure and add enough water to measure 3/4 cup liquid. Pour into a small saucepan and bring to a boil. Remove from the heat and add the gelatin, stirring until dissolved. Stir in the port and lemon juice. Chill until partially set. Fold in the pears and raspberries with their juices. Pour into a 6-cup mold or 6 individual molds. Chill until firm.

Mango Salsa

Yield: 4 servings

Accompany grilled fish or roasted pork with this side dish. As an alternative, serve as a dip for shrimp or corn chips.

1 jalapeño chile
1 large ripe mango, peeled and coarsely chopped
1/2 cup finely chopped onion
1/4 cup fresh lime juice
1/4 cup chopped fresh cilantro
1/4 teaspoon cumin
1/4 teaspoon salt

Roast the jalapeño chile over a gas flame or under a broiler until the skin is charred on all sides. Remove and discard the blackened skin, using plastic gloves to protect your hands. Seed and finely chop the chile. Combine the mango, onion, lime juice, cilantro, cumin, salt and 1/2 to 3/4 of the chile in a bowl and mix well. Let stand in the refrigerator for 1 hour. Add more of the jalapeño chile for a hotter taste. Serve cold or at room temperature.

The Palo Alto Men's Club

In the early 1930s, luncheon sales were notoriously slow on Mondays. The Restaurant needed at least forty customers just to break even.

Twelve men—prominent community businessmen, doctors, and Stanford professors—came to lunch on Mondays quite often. The volunteers referred to them as "the boys."

In an effort to ensure continued business from "the boys," the Auxiliary began to give them their lunches for only fifty cents. As was hoped, "the boys" came to lunch regularly on Mondays for many years. That was the beginning of the Palo Alto Men's Club.

Tantalizing Tomatillo Salsa

Serve this refreshing and flavorful salsa as a condiment with grilled fish, as a cooling side dish with spicy foods, or as a dip for corn chips.

Yield: 1 1/2 cups

> 3 tomatillos, husks and stems removed, finely chopped
> 1/2 to 3/4 cup chopped seeded peeled cucumber
> 1 teaspoon finely chopped lemon zest
> 2 to 3 tablespoons fresh lime juice, or to taste
> 1 jalapeño chile, seeded and minced
> 1/4 teaspoon kosher salt
> 1 large ripe avocado, diced
> 1 cup chopped cilantro (about 1/2 bunch)

Combine the tomatillos, cucumber, lemon zest, lime juice, 1/2 of the jalapeño chile and the salt in a medium bowl and mix well. Add more of the jalapeño chile as desired for a hotter taste. Stir in the avocado and cilantro just before serving. Serve cold or at room temperature.

Tomatillos

Tomatillos resemble small green tomatoes enclosed in a papery husk that must be removed prior to use. When ripened to a yellow-white color, tomatillos become very sweet.

Although unfamiliar to many, tomatillos are frequently used in Mexican cooking. When eaten raw, their tangy flavor perfectly complements salsas or salads. They may also be cooked, either alone or with other ingredients.

Tomatillos can readily be found in the produce section of almost any market. Purchase small, firm ones, free of defects, with a light brown, fresh-looking papery husk.

Woman with Children

Fresh Cranberry Relish

Yield: 3 cups

This favorite is the most flavorful condiment we could find to enhance the flavor of your holiday turkey or that leftover turkey sandwich.

    1 Granny Smith or other tart green apple, peeled, cored and finely diced
    $1^2/_3$ cups sugar
    $^1/_4$ cup honey
    $^1/_4$ cup freshly squeezed orange juice
    Grated zest of 1 orange
    1 tablespoon brandy
    $^1/_4$ teaspoon cinnamon
    12 ounces fresh cranberries

Combine the apple, sugar, honey, orange juice, orange zest, brandy and cinnamon in a saucepan over medium heat. Cook until the sugar is dissolved, stirring constantly. Add the cranberries. Cook until the cranberries have popped open and the mixture is slightly thickened, stirring constantly. Let stand until cool. Store in the refrigerator.

Curried Fruit

Yield: 6 to 8 servings

Use jars of salad fruit found in the produce section of your market—not canned fruit cocktail. This dish is good served with roasted or barbecued pork, chicken, or turkey.

    1 (24-ounce) jar mixed salad fruit
    $^1/_4$ cup ($^1/_2$ stick) butter
    $^1/_4$ cup chutney
    1 tablespoon curry powder
    2 cups fresh or frozen cantaloupe or honeydew melon balls

Drain the salad fruit, reserving $^3/_4$ cup syrup. Combine the butter, chutney, curry powder and reserved syrup in a saucepan and bring to a boil. Cook for 10 minutes or until thickened. Stir in the salad fruit and melon balls. Chill, covered, until serving time. Let stand for 30 minutes before serving.

Apple Cider Sauce

Yield: 1½ cups

A slightly sweet, yet pungent, sauce that will add a finishing touch to chicken, lamb, pork, turkey, or meatballs.

> ¼ cup (½ stick) butter
> 1 tablespoon vegetable oil
> 1 onion, finely chopped
> 1 garlic clove, minced
> 1 teaspoon curry powder, or to taste
> ½ teaspoon salt
> 3 tablespoons all-purpose flour
> 1½ cups apple cider
> 1 large unpeeled tart green apple, cored and finely chopped

Heat the butter and oil in a heavy skillet over medium heat. Add the onion and sauté until almost caramelized. Sprinkle the garlic, curry powder, salt and flour over the onion. Cook for 1 to 2 minutes, stirring constantly. Whisk in the apple cider, stirring until smooth. Add the apple. Cook for 10 to 15 minutes or until the apple is very soft. Thin the sauce with additional apple cider if necessary.

Spiced Cranberry Sauce

Yield: 3¾ cups

This traditional and colorful topping, served hot, will complement your holiday turkey, pork roast, or meatballs.

> 1 (16-ounce) can whole cranberries
> 1 (12-ounce) bottle tomato chili sauce
> ½ cup red wine
> 3 tablespoons fresh lemon juice
> 2 tablespoons sugar
> ⅛ teaspoon garlic salt

Heat the cranberries in a large saucepan over low heat, mashing the cranberries coarsely. Add the chili sauce, red wine, lemon juice, sugar and garlic salt and mix well. Cook until the sugar dissolves, stirring constantly. Serve the sauce hot.

Salmon Cream Sauce

Serve this versatile sauce over angel hair pasta or bow-tie pasta.
Or try it over toast points, rice, or white fish fillets.

Yield: 2³/4 cups or 3 to 4 servings

3 tablespoons butter
¹/2 cup finely chopped red bell pepper (about 1 small pepper)
¹/4 cup minced shallots (about 3 large cloves)
1¹/2 tablespoons all-purpose flour
2 cups milk
1 cup flaked smoked or kippered salmon (not lox style)
2 tablespoons fresh lemon juice
1 teaspoon salt, or to taste
1 teaspoon paprika
¹/2 teaspoon Tabasco sauce
Freshly ground pepper to taste

Melt the butter in a 2-quart saucepan over medium heat. Add the bell pepper and shallots and sauté until the shallots are translucent. Sprinkle with the flour. Cook for 1 to 2 minutes, stirring constantly. Whisk in the milk and bring to a boil. Reduce the heat and simmer for 4 to 5 minutes or until the sauce thickens. Reduce the heat to low. Stir in the salmon, lemon juice, salt, paprika, Tabasco sauce and pepper. Cook over very low heat a little longer to concentrate the flavors if desired. Garnish each serving with a chiffonade of fresh basil.

Totes for Tots

Over the years, the Palo Alto Auxiliary has been blessed with a vast array of members possessing many diverse talents. We not only treasure and utilize these members for their versatile culinary skills, but their creative sewing skills as well.

No matter how much we might wish otherwise, some sick children must remain in the hospital over the holidays. For these kids, the Palo Alto Auxiliary Tote Bag Committee produces approximately six dozen brightly colored fabric totes, which are then filled with books and toys.

Sewn by members, with some enthusiastic help from non-members, these tote bags, donated every year, are a most welcome "perker-upper" for the children too ill to be at home for the holidays. They are just one more traditional gift of love from our dedicated and talented members.

Marinated Mushrooms

Yield: about 36 servings

Serve as an appetizer or as a sandwich accompaniment. Or add to an antipasto platter alongside chopped tomatoes, black olives, and marinated artichoke hearts. These are mouthwatering and very flavorful!

3/4 pound fresh small button mushrooms
2/3 cup olive oil
1/2 cup red wine vinegar
2 teaspoons Italian seasoning
1 1/2 teaspoons seasoned salt
2 garlic cloves, minced
1/4 cup chopped fresh Italian parsley

Place the mushrooms in a bowl, a jar with a tight-fitting lid or a sealable plastic bag. Combine the olive oil, vinegar, Italian seasoning, seasoned salt, garlic and parsley in a bowl and mix well. Pour the mixture over the mushrooms. Chill for 8 hours, stirring occasionally. Remove from the refrigerator and let stand for 1 hour before serving; drain, reserving the marinade. Store uneaten mushrooms in the marinade in the refrigerator.

Swedish Meatballs

Yield: 45 to 50 servings

Serve meatballs as an appetizer in Apple Cider Sauce (page 113) or in Spiced Cranberry Sauce (page 113). Alternatively, add them to your favorite tomato sauce and serve over pasta.

1 pound twice-ground beef
1/2 pound ground pork
1/2 pound ground veal
1 onion, grated
1 potato, peeled, cooked and mashed
1/2 cup milk
Salt and pepper to taste

Line a large baking pan with parchment paper. Preheat the oven to 400 degrees. Combine the ground beef, ground pork, ground veal, onion, potato and milk in a large bowl and mix well. Add the salt and pepper. Cook a small amount of the meat mixture in a skillet and taste for seasoning. Adjust the seasoning if necessary. Shape into 1-inch balls using the large end of a melon baller. Place in the prepared baking pan. Bake for 20 to 25 minutes or until cooked through, shaking the pan every 5 minutes so the meatballs will retain their shape and brown evenly.

The meatballs may be shaped a day ahead of use. Store, tightly covered, in the refrigerator and cook just before serving. Alternatively, cook and freeze for later use. When ready to serve, let the meatballs stand at room temperature, and then heat at 400 degrees for 10 minutes.

East-West Chicken Wings

Yield: 48 servings

Where East meets West, enjoy the fusion of exotic flavors with homegrown ingredients.

24 chicken wings, or 48 drumettes
1 cup soy sauce
1/2 cup dry sherry
1 tablespoon brown sugar
3 large garlic cloves, minced
1/2 cup chopped green onions
1 tablespoon minced fresh ginger, or
    1/2 teaspoon ground ginger
1 tablespoon vegetable oil
1 cup all-purpose flour
3/4 cup freshly grated Parmesan cheese

Cut the chicken wings into halves at the main joints. Cut off the wing tips and discard. Combine the soy sauce, sherry, brown sugar, garlic, green onions, ginger and oil in a bowl and whisk until blended. Add the chicken and toss to coat. Chill, covered, for 2 to 24 hours.

Preheat the oven to 350 degrees. Grease 2 baking sheets. Combine the flour and cheese in a large shallow dish. Remove the chicken wings from the marinade and drain well. Discard the marinade. Add the chicken, 1 piece at a time, to the flour mixture and roll to coat. Shake off any excess flour and arrange in a single layer on the baking sheets, making sure that the chicken pieces do not touch each other. Bake for 30 minutes. Turn the chicken over and bake an additional 15 minutes or until tender and cooked through. Drain on paper towels. Serve hot or at room temperature.

Tortilla Pinwheels

Yield: about 40 pinwheels

Expect a lively and refreshing southwestern flair from these circular sandwiches filled with chiles and several types of cheeses, then topped with salsa.

1 cup sour cream
8 ounces cream cheese, softened
3/4 cup (3 ounces) shredded Cheddar cheese
1/4 cup (1 ounce) shredded Monterey
    Jack cheese
1/2 cup finely chopped green onions
1/4 cup chopped black olives, drained
1 (2-ounce) jar chopped pimentos, drained
1/4 cup chopped green chiles
10 to 12 (6-inch) tortillas

Combine the sour cream, cream cheese, Cheddar cheese and Monterey Jack cheese in a bowl and mix well. Stir in the green onions, olives, pimentos and chiles. Spread over the tortillas, leaving a 1/2-inch edge. Roll up the tortillas and wrap each in plastic wrap. Chill for at least 3 hours. Trim the ends and slice each roll into 1-inch pieces. Arrange the pinwheels on a serving platter and top each with a dollop of salsa, or place a bowl of salsa in the center of the platter for dipping.

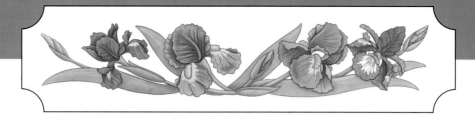

Spinach Wraps

Yield: 40 roll-ups

Nutritious and colorful spirals, filled with a hearty vegetable and cream cheese mixture. It looks beautiful and tastes even better. Handy to have in the freezer for a quick sandwich or appetizer.

1 (10-ounce) package frozen chopped spinach,
   thawed, squeezed dry and rechopped
8 ounces cream cheese, softened
$1/2$ cup grated Parmesan cheese
2 teaspoons creamy horseradish
2 tablespoons mayonnaise
$1/8$ teaspoon allspice
1 teaspoon salt
$1/2$ teaspoon pepper
1 (15-ounce) can white kidney beans
1 tablespoon unseasoned rice wine vinegar
2 teaspoons honey
$1/2$ teaspoon thyme leaves
$1/2$ teaspoon salt
10 (6-inch) flour tortillas
$1/2$ cup finely chopped green onions
$1/2$ cup finely chopped Italian parsley
$1/3$ cup chopped roasted red bell pepper or pimento

    Combine the spinach, cream cheese, Parmesan cheese, horseradish, mayonnaise, allspice, 1 teaspoon salt and the pepper in a food processor fitted with a steel blade. Process until smooth. Drain the kidney beans, reserving the liquid. Rinse the beans in cold water; drain. Combine the beans, vinegar, honey, thyme and $1/2$ teaspoon salt in a small bowl. Mash the bean mixture, adding enough of the reserved bean liquid to reach a spreading consistency. Spread $2^{1}/2$ tablespoons of the spinach mixture over each tortilla, leaving a 1-inch edge. Spread 1 tablespoon of the bean mixture over the spinach mixture. Sprinkle some of the green onions, parsley and bell pepper over the spinach mixture. Roll up the tortillas and place them on a baking sheet seam side down. Chill, tightly covered, until serving time, or freeze on the baking sheet and store the tortillas, individually wrapped in foil, in freezer bags in the freezer. Let the frozen roll-ups stand at room temperature for at least 2 hours. Slice end portions to even, then slice each roll-up into 4 pieces and serve at room temperature.

Murray House

Beef Tenderloin with Horseradish Sauce

Yield: 4 to 6 servings

This dish is guaranteed to be a hit at your next dinner party or buffet. The leftover sauce perfectly complements roast beef sandwiches, carrots, or asparagus.

1¹/2 pounds beef tenderloin
    (filet mignon roast)
1 tablespoon finely chopped fresh rosemary
1 tablespoon cracked pepper
¹/4 cup balsamic vinegar
2 tablespoons butter, softened
1 teaspoon salt
Horseradish Sauce

Wine Note: *This beef tenderloin, with its flavorful horseradish sauce, can stand up to a big wine. Here one of the Rhône varietals, such as syrah, would be a good choice.*

Remove the fat and silver skin from the beef. Combine the rosemary and pepper and rub over the beef. Let stand for 2 hours at room temperature. Preheat the oven to 500 degrees. Brush the vinegar over the beef. Spread the butter over the surface and sprinkle with the salt. Place the roast on a rack in a roasting pan. Place the pan in the preheated oven and lower the temperature to 400 degrees. Roast for 25 to 30 minutes or to 120 degrees on an instant-read thermometer for medium-rare. Remove from the oven and let stand for 10 minutes before slicing. Cut across the grain into thin strips. Pour the pan juices over the beef. Serve hot, cold or at room temperature with Horseradish Sauce.

Horseradish Sauce

Yield: 1³/4 cups

³/4 cup mayonnaise
³/4 cup sour cream
3 tablespoons finely chopped fresh chives or
    green onion tops
2 tablespoons prepared horseradish
¹/8 teaspoon freshly ground pepper

Combine the mayonnaise, sour cream, chives, horseradish and pepper in a small bowl and mix well.

Flank Steak with Caramelized Onions

Yield: 4 to 6 servings

Forget the steak sauce! Onions sautéed to a golden brown provide all the flavor and juice required to make this steak entrée a winner. You will need one hour or more refrigeration time.

Caramelized Onions
2 large yellow or white onions, thinly sliced
1 large red onion, thinly sliced
1/4 cup olive oil
1 tablespoon balsamic vinegar
Salt and pepper to taste

Steak
3 large garlic cloves, minced
2 tablespoons olive oil
2 tablespoons chopped fresh parsley
1 tablespoon lemon juice
1 teaspoon salt
1 teaspoon coarsely ground pepper
2 pounds flank steak, trimmed and scored

For the onions, cook the onions in the olive oil in a large skillet over medium-low heat for 25 to 30 minutes or until soft, stirring occasionally. Increase the heat to medium and stir in the vinegar. Sauté until the onions are a deep golden color, stirring frequently. Add the salt and pepper. Serve immediately or store and reheat just before serving.

For the steak, combine the garlic, olive oil, parsley, lemon juice, salt and pepper in a small bowl and mix to a paste consistency. Place the steak in a shallow pan. Rub the garlic mixture over both sides of the steak. Chill, covered, for at least 1 hour. Grill over hot coals for 5 to 7 minutes on each side for medium-rare or broil 4 inches from the heat source for 4 to 5 minutes on each side. Remove the steak to a platter and tent with foil. Let stand for 5 to 10 minutes before slicing. Cut across the grain into very thin slices. Serve with Caramelized Onions.

Wine Note: *This dish clearly has a sweet touch, and while merlot has lost some of its popularity, it is the obvious choice for this creation.*

Flank Steak Sandwiches

Make open-face sandwiches with leftover flank steak.

Slice French bread on the diagonal. Heat 1 tablespoon olive oil and 1 tablespoon butter in a large nonstick skillet over medium heat. Add bread slices, turning to coat both sides with oil. Toast bread on both sides. While bread is browning, put very thin slices of leftover flank steak and caramelized onions on one side of the skillet to heat. To serve, pile meat and onions on top of each bread slice.

This sandwich is good served with marinated red bell peppers or pimentos.

Oven Pot Roast

Yield: 6 to 8 servings

This recipe dates back to World War II, when rump roast required fewer food stamps than other cuts of meat. Long slow cooking produces a tender roast with lots of rich gravy. Oven-roasted carrots and potatoes make a perfect accompaniment.

1/3 cup bacon drippings
1/2 cup all-purpose flour
2 tablespoons sugar
2 teaspoons dry mustard
1/2 teaspoon celery seeds
2 tablespoons salt
2 teaspoons pepper
3 pounds rump roast
1 (28-ounce) can stewed tomatoes
3 large onions, sliced

Preheat the oven to 350 degrees. Combine the bacon drippings, flour, sugar, dry mustard, celery seeds, salt and pepper in a bowl and mix to a paste consistency. Rub over the surface of the roast. Place the roast on a rack in a roasting pan with a tight-fitting cover. Roast, uncovered, for 20 minutes or until the roast is a rich brown. Lower the oven temperature to 300 degrees. Strain the tomatoes through a sieve. Add the strained juice to the pan, reserving the tomatoes for another use. Add the onions. Roast, covered, for 2 1/2 to 3 hours or until tender, or to 170 degrees on a meat thermometer.

Wine Note: *Cabernet sauvignon or Bordeaux varietal blends would be the perfect accompaniment for this classic comfort food.*

Surviving World War II

World War II created a significant impact on Allied Arts Guild Restaurant. Many members moved out of the area with their military husbands. Others joined the American Red Cross. Fewer people were dining out because of gas rationing. Only nine attended the first meal after rationing started.

Food rationing imposed on families became more severe than on the Restaurant, and people soon realized that entertaining at home could be more expensive than lunching out. Consequently, they began to carpool, enjoy lunch at the Restaurant, and save their precious rations for home meals. Soon, the customer count exceeded pre-war figures.

Although the lunchroom was not rationed as severely as families, it was difficult to obtain supplies. Creative cooking became the order of the day. Our volunteers met the challenge, and we survived World War II.

Little did they know the results of their tenacity and dedication would blossom into today's successful restaurant.

Lamb Tarragon

Yield: 4 to 6 servings

Turn this recipe into a curry dish by adding one tablespoon curry powder in place of the tarragon. Serve either version over rice or noodles.

2 pounds lamb shoulder, cut into $1/2$-inch cubes
Salt and pepper to taste
$1^1/2$ tablespoons olive oil
1 tablespoon butter
1 small onion, chopped
1 tablespoon all-purpose flour
$1^1/2$ to 2 cups chicken broth, heated
$1/2$ cup dry white wine
1 teaspoon dried tarragon, or 1 tablespoon minced fresh tarragon
$1/2$ cup sour cream
Hot cooked rice, noodles or garlic mashed potatoes

Wine Note: *Lamb and tarragon must be one of the happiest food pairings in the world. This classic recipe begs for a great red burgundy, which is made entirely from the pinot noir grape, grown in the Burgundy region east of Paris.*

Sprinkle the lamb with salt and pepper. Heat a little of the olive oil in a large skillet over medium-high heat. Add a layer of the lamb to the pan without crowding and brown on all sides. Remove the lamb to a dish. Brown the remaining lamb, adding more of the olive oil as needed. Reduce the heat to medium-low. Melt the butter in the skillet. Add the onion and sauté until translucent. Sprinkle the flour over the onion. Cook for 2 minutes, stirring constantly. Add $1/2$ cup of the chicken broth, the wine and tarragon, stirring until smooth. Bring to a boil. Reduce the heat and simmer, uncovered, until the sauce is thick and reduced by half, stirring occasionally. Return the lamb and any accumulated juices to the pan. Stir in 1 cup of the chicken broth. Simmer, covered, for 30 minutes or until the lamb is tender, stirring occasionally and adding additional broth if the sauce reduces too much. Add the sour cream just before serving and heat gently. Adjust the seasonings. Serve over rice, noodles or garlic mashed Yukon Gold potatoes. Garnish with chopped fresh tarragon.

Old World Greek Moussaka

Yield: 6 to 8 servings

The scent of aromatic spices permeates the air when this ethnic favorite is baking. It may be assembled one day before serving and topped with the béchamel sauce just before baking.

Meat Sauce

1$^1/_2$ pounds ground lamb or ground beef
1 tablespoon olive oil
1 cup chopped onion
2 garlic cloves, minced
1 (8-ounce) can tomato sauce
$^1/_4$ cup red wine
2 tablespoons chopped fresh parsley
$^1/_2$ teaspoon basil
$^1/_4$ teaspoon oregano
$^1/_4$ teaspoon each cinnamon and nutmeg
1 teaspoon salt
$^1/_2$ teaspoon pepper

Béchamel Sauce

$^1/_3$ cup butter, melted
$^1/_3$ cup all-purpose flour
1$^1/_4$ cups milk, heated
1$^1/_4$ cups half-and-half, heated
$^1/_2$ teaspoon salt
$^1/_4$ teaspoon nutmeg
4 egg yolks, beaten
$^1/_4$ cup grated Parmesan cheese

Moussaka

3 eggplant, cut into $^1/_2$-inch slices
Olive oil
Paprika

For the meat sauce, brown the lamb in a large skillet, stirring until crumbly; drain. Remove the lamb to a dish. Add the olive oil, onion and garlic to the skillet. Sauté over medium heat until the onion is translucent. Return the lamb to the skillet. Stir in the tomato sauce, red wine, parsley, basil, oregano, cinnamon, nutmeg, salt and pepper. Simmer for 20 minutes, stirring occasionally.

For the béchamel sauce, melt the butter in a large saucepan and whisk in the flour. Cook for 1 to 2 minutes, stirring constantly. Whisk in the milk and half-and-half slowly, stirring until smooth. Bring to a boil. Reduce the heat and simmer until the sauce thickens, stirring frequently. Add the salt and nutmeg. Stir a small amount of the sauce into the beaten egg yolks; stir the egg yolks into the hot sauce. Cook until thickened, stirring constantly. Stir in the cheese.

For the moussaka, grease a baking sheet. Preheat the oven to 400 degrees. Brush the eggplant slices with olive oil on both sides. Place on the prepared baking sheet in 1 layer. Bake for 20 minutes or until tender. Grease a 9×12-inch baking pan. Reduce the oven temperature to 350 degrees. Layer $^1/_2$ of the eggplant and $^1/_2$ of the meat sauce in the prepared baking pan. Repeat the layers. Spread the béchamel sauce evenly over the meat sauce. Sprinkle with paprika. Bake, uncovered, for 1 hour or until hot and bubbly. Let stand, covered with foil, for 10 minutes before serving.

Wine Note: *If you have not tried any of the new Greek wines lately, you would be amazed at the quality. Gone are the bitter retsinas of the past, and in their place are many marvelous new wines. Ask your wine merchant about a Greek wine to pair with this staple of Greek cuisine.*

Roasted Pork Tenderloin with Red Currant Sauce

Yield: 4 to 6 servings

Succulent pork roast, stuffed with a walnut-curry filling and served with a sweet and spicy sauce, makes a feast fit for a king.

3/4 cup walnuts, chopped
2 tablespoons butter
1 tablespoon plus 1 teaspoon vegetable oil
1 large garlic clove, coarsely chopped
1 teaspoon curry powder
1 1/2 pounds pork tenderloin, trimmed
1 1/2 teaspoons ground coriander
1 teaspoon ground cumin
1 1/2 teaspoons salt
1/4 teaspoon pepper
Red Currant Sauce

Wine Note: *This fabulous creation cries out for a great white burgundy. Although it is expensive, a batard-montrachet would be superb.*

Grease a 9×13-inch baking pan. Preheat the oven to 350 degrees. Cook the walnuts in the butter in a skillet over medium heat for 1 to 2 minutes or until lightly toasted. Combine the walnuts, oil, garlic and curry powder in a food processor and process until finely ground. Slice the pork tenderloin lengthwise to within 1/2 inch of the bottom; spread the 2 halves open like a book. Spread the walnut mixture evenly down the center. Tie the halves together with kitchen twine or secure them with skewers. Combine the coriander, cumin, salt and pepper in a small bowl and mix well. Rub over all surfaces of the pork. Place the tenderloin in the prepared baking pan seam side up. Bake for 30 minutes or to 150 to 160 degrees on a meat thermometer. Let stand, loosely covered with foil, for 10 minutes. Cut across the grain into 1/2-inch slices. Top each serving with Red Currant Sauce.

Red Currant Sauce

Yield: 1 1/2 cups

1 (12-ounce) jar red currant jelly
1 shallot, finely chopped
2 tablespoons dry sherry
1 tablespoon apple cider vinegar
1/2 teaspoon ginger
1/4 teaspoon red pepper flakes

Combine the red currant jelly, shallot, sherry, vinegar, ginger and red pepper flakes in a small saucepan and mix well. Bring to a boil over moderate heat. Simmer for 5 minutes.

Ham Tortillas

Yield: 8 servings

Savor each irresistible bite of these roll-ups filled with chopped ham and covered with a creamy rich white sauce. Try substituting homemade crêpes (see page 140) for the tortillas.

6 tablespoons butter
3 tablespoons all-purpose flour
2 cups milk, heated
1 teaspoon salt, or to taste
1 tablespoon butter
8 ounces mushrooms, sliced
1/4 cup finely chopped shallots
2 garlic cloves, finely chopped
2 tablespoons dry white wine
1/2 teaspoon dried thyme leaves
1/4 teaspoon pepper
2/3 pound cooked low-salt ham, cubed
8 (6-inch) flour tortillas
1/4 cup dry white wine
1 cup (4 ounces) shredded Gruyère cheese,
    or a mix of Parmesan cheese, asiago
    cheese and fontina cheese
Paprika

Wine Note: *Try a chardonnay or, even better, a California viognier, which is one of the finest of the white Rhône varietals.*

Melt 6 tablespoons butter in a medium saucepan over medium heat. Stir in the flour. Cook for 1 to 2 minutes, stirring constantly. Whisk in the milk and bring to a boil. Reduce the heat and simmer until smooth and thick, stirring constantly. Add the salt. Melt 1 tablespoon butter in a large skillet. Add the mushrooms, shallots and garlic and sauté until tender. Stir in 2 tablespoons wine, the thyme and pepper. Cook until the liquid has evaporated. Remove from the heat and add the ham. Stir in 1/2 to 2/3 cup of the white sauce, or enough to make a thick filling.

Grease a 9×13-inch baking pan. Preheat the oven to 350 degrees. Spoon 2/3 cup of the filling onto each tortilla and roll to enclose the filling. Place seam side down in the prepared pan. Stir 1/4 cup wine into the remaining sauce to thin. Pour over the tortillas and top with the cheese. Sprinkle with paprika. Bake for 30 minutes or until hot and bubbly. Garnish with a mix of chopped red, orange and yellow bell peppers.

Polenta and Sausage

Yield: 6 to 8 servings

For a soft and creamy polenta, make this classic northern Italian specialty just prior to serving. Spread any leftover polenta in a pan and chill. It will thicken and harden. Slice the polenta and toast it in a skillet with olive oil or on the grill for a great side dish.

Sausage Topping

1 pound Italian sausage (hot, mild or a mix),
    casings removed and sausage chopped
2 tablespoons olive oil
1 pound button mushrooms, cleaned
    and sliced
1 (28-ounce) can crushed tomatoes
1 teaspoon salt
1/4 teaspoon pepper

Polenta

2 cups water
2 cups cornmeal
6 cups water
1 tablespoon salt
1/4 cup (1/2 stick) butter (optional)
2/3 cup grated Parmesan cheese or Romano
    cheese (optional)

For the topping, brown the sausage in a large skillet over medium heat, stirring until crumbly; drain and remove to a dish. Heat the olive oil in the skillet. Add the mushrooms and sauté until tender. Return the sausage to the skillet. Add the tomatoes, salt and pepper. Simmer, covered, for 20 to 30 minutes or until the sauce thickens. Adjust the seasonings.

For the polenta, combine 2 cups water and the cornmeal in a small bowl and mix well. Bring 6 cups water to a boil in a large nonstick saucepan. Add the salt. Stir the cornmeal mixture slowly into the boiling water. Cook until the mixture thickens, stirring constantly with a long-handled wooden spoon. Reduce the heat. Cook, covered, for 10 minutes or until the polenta is soft and creamy. Stir in the butter and cheese. Spoon the hot polenta onto individual plates and top with the sausage mixture. Garnish with additional cheese.

Wine Note: *For this Italian recipe, there are three recommendations, one for each of the suggested sausages: hot: chianti; hot plus mild: barolo; mild: montepulciano (the grape, not the village).*

Indonesian Chicken Satay

Yield: 34 appetizer servings

Satays, a gift from Indonesia, consist of small cubes of marinated meat or poultry, broiled or grilled, then dipped into a spicy peanut sauce. Serve them as a snack, appetizer, or main entrée. They need four to twenty-four hours of marinating.

2 tablespoons peanut oil
1 tablespoon sesame oil
3/4 cup chopped onion
2 1/2 tablespoons minced garlic
1 tablespoon grated fresh ginger
1 1/2 tablespoons rice wine vinegar
1 1/2 tablespoons light brown sugar
1/2 cup creamy peanut butter
1/4 cup ketchup
1/4 cup soy sauce
2 1/2 tablespoons fresh lime juice
3/4 teaspoon ground coriander
3/4 teaspoon freshly ground pepper
1/8 teaspoon chili oil, or to taste
1/4 cup mayonnaise
2 pounds boneless skinless chicken breast halves, tendons removed, cut into 1-inch strips (or substitute pork or beef)

Heat the peanut oil and sesame oil in a large skillet over low heat. Add the onion, garlic and ginger. Cook for 3 to 4 minutes or until the onion is translucent, stirring constantly. Stir in the vinegar and brown sugar. Cook until the brown sugar dissolves. Remove from the heat. Add the peanut butter, ketchup, soy sauce, lime juice, coriander, pepper and chili oil. Pour into the bowl of a food processor and process until smooth. Combine 3/4 cup of the peanut butter mixture and the mayonnaise in a small bowl. Chill the peanut sauce, covered, until serving time. Combine the remaining purée with the chicken strips in a bowl and mix well. Marinate, covered, in the refrigerator for at least 4 hours.

Grease a large baking sheet. Preheat the broiler. Place the marinated chicken strips on the prepared baking sheet. Broil for 6 minutes on each side or until golden brown and crisp. Let stand until cool enough to handle. Cut the strips into 1-inch cubes. Toss the chicken cubes in the peanut sauce in a small bowl. Arrange the satay cubes on a serving platter and serve with wooden picks. Serve hot or at room temperature.

Wine Note: *The wines of Germany offer a variety of levels of sweetness. The acidity of a classic German kabinet or spätlese would be a perfect pairing with this spicy creation.*

Crêpe Suizas

Yield: 10 crêpes

Crêpes were a popular luncheon entrée during the 1970s and 1980s. Try substituting flour tortillas for the crêpes to create a Mexican version of a French classic.

> 5 cups shredded cooked chicken
> 1 (7-ounce) can diced mild green chiles, drained
> 1¹/₂ cups sour cream
> 1 teaspoon salt
> 10 crêpes (see recipe at right) or 10 (7-inch) flour tortillas
> 1 (16-ounce) jar thick medium-spiced salsa
> 10 (2×4-inch) slices Monterey Jack cheese
> ²/₃ cup sour cream, thinned with 3 tablespoons milk
> ¹/₄ cup sliced black olives

Grease individual ramekins or a 9×13-inch baking dish. Preheat the oven to 350 degrees. Combine the chicken, chiles, 1¹/₂ cups sour cream and salt in a large bowl and mix well. Spread ¹/₃ to ¹/₂ cup of the chicken filling down the center of each crêpe. Top with 1¹/₂ tablespoons of the salsa. Fold the sides of the crêpe over the filling. Place the crêpes in the prepared ramekins seam side down. Top each crêpe with a slice of the cheese. Cover the dishes with a tent of greased foil. Bake for 25 to 30 minutes. Remove the foil. Bake for 5 minutes longer. Top each crêpe with a dollop of the thinned sour cream and a few black olive slices. Pass additional salsa.

Wine Note: *While a dark Mexican beer seems like the obvious choice, tequila with salt and lime would be terrific.*

Basic Crêpes

Yield: 18 crêpes

> 2 cups all-purpose flour
> ¹/₂ teaspoon salt
> 1 cup cold water
> 1 cup cold milk
> 4 eggs, beaten
> ¹/₄ cup (¹/₂ stick) butter, melted and cooled
> Vegetable oil or butter

Combine the flour and salt in a mixing bowl. Whisk the water, milk, eggs and butter slowly into the flour mixture, beating until smooth, or combine the ingredients in a blender and process for 1 minute. Chill in the refrigerator for 2 hours or longer. Heat a 7-inch heavy-bottomed or nonstick skillet over medium-high heat. Brush the skillet with oil. Heat until the oil begins to smoke. Pour ¹/₄ cup of the batter into the skillet. Tilt the skillet to spread the batter in a thin layer over the bottom. Cook for 1 to 2 minutes or until the top bubbles and the edges are brown. Loosen the crêpe and turn it over. Cook for 30 seconds or until golden on the bottom. Repeat the procedure with the remaining batter. Stack the cooked crêpes between sheets of waxed paper.

Note: *Use a second preheated nonstick skillet to speed up the process of making crêpes. When the first side has set, turn the crêpe into a second skillet to complete cooking while you start making the next crêpe in the first skillet. Make crêpes ahead and refrigerate or freeze. When making, place waxed paper between each crêpe. Cool and bundle several crêpes together in foil. Place in a tightly sealed plastic freezer bag. Chill or freeze until ready to use. As an alternative, fill crêpes with cooked fruits or fresh berries and top with a sweet sauce for an easy, tasty, and impressive dessert.*

Turkey Velvet Supreme

Yield: 6 to 8 servings

This crowd-pleasing casserole was frequently served at the Restaurant during the holidays when preparation time was at a minimum and reservations were at a maximum.

1 tablespoon butter
1 pound mushrooms, sliced
1/4 cup (1/2 stick) butter
1/4 cup flour
2 1/2 cups chicken broth, heated
1 teaspoon poultry seasoning
1/4 cup dry sherry
Salt and pepper to taste
3 tablespoons butter, melted
1/2 cup dry unseasoned bread crumbs
1 teaspoon paprika
4 1/2 cups cubed roasted turkey or
   deli-roasted chicken
1 (14-ounce) can water-packed artichoke
   hearts, rinsed, drained and quartered
2 cups (8 ounces) shredded Swiss cheese
Dry unseasoned bread crumbs

Wine Note: *The artichoke hearts in this dish give it an earthy character. Here an Alsatian pinot gris or a chilled light pinot noir will serve.*

Grease a 9×13-inch baking dish. Preheat the oven to 350 degrees. Melt 1 tablespoon butter in a small skillet. Add the mushrooms and sauté until tender; drain, reserving any liquid. Melt 1/4 cup butter in a small saucepan over medium heat and stir in the flour. Cook for 1 to 2 minutes, stirring constantly. Whisk in the chicken broth and poultry seasoning. Bring to a boil. Increase the heat and simmer until the sauce thickens, stirring constantly. Stir in the sherry, salt and pepper. Reduce the heat and simmer for a few minutes longer. Stir in the reserved mushroom liquid to thin the sauce if necessary. Combine 3 tablespoons melted butter with the bread crumbs and paprika in a small bowl and mix well.

Spread 1/3 of the sauce in the prepared baking dish. Layer the turkey, artichokes, mushrooms and cheese over the sauce. Top with the remaining sauce. Poke holes through the layers using a fork, allowing the sauce to seep downward. Sprinkle bread crumbs evenly over the top. Bake for 30 to 35 minutes or until hot and bubbly. Serve in individual casserole dishes. Garnish with finely chopped fresh parsley or chives.

Turkey and Rice Casserole

Yield: 6 servings

Don't wait for leftover turkey to make this Restaurant favorite. Try substituting deli-roasted chicken instead. Either way, the family will ask for a repeat performance.

1 (10-ounce) can condensed cream of chicken soup
1 1/2 cups sour cream
1 (4-ounce) can diced mild green chiles, drained
2 tablespoons finely chopped green bell peppers
2 tablespoons sliced green onions
1 teaspoon oregano
1/2 teaspoon garlic powder
1/2 teaspoon pepper
1/4 teaspoon salt, or to taste
2 cups cooked rice
1 1/2 cups (6 ounces) shredded Monterey Jack cheese
2 cups thinly sliced small zucchini
2 cups cubed roasted turkey or deli-roasted chicken
1 (15-ounce) can diced tomatoes, drained

Grease a 9×13-inch baking pan. Preheat the oven to 350 degrees. Combine the soup, sour cream, chiles, bell peppers, green onions, oregano, garlic powder, pepper and salt in a bowl and mix well. Remove 1 cup of the soup mixture to a small bowl; add the rice and mix well. Spread the rice mixture evenly in the prepared pan. Layer 1/3 of the cheese, all of the zucchini and all of the turkey over the rice mixture. Continue layering with 1 cup of the soup mixture, 1/3 of the cheese, all of the tomatoes, the remaining soup mixture and the remaining cheese. Bake for 40 to 50 minutes or until hot and bubbly. Let stand, covered tightly with foil, for 5 to 10 minutes before cutting into squares. Garnish with chopped fresh parsley.

Wine Note: *While chardonnay is the obvious choice, you might want to challenge your palate with a slightly sweet demi-sec Loire wine. The white wines of the Loire valley are made from chenin blanc, one of the most misunderstood grapes of France.*

Recipes Changing Over Time

All the recipes served at the Restaurant were contributed by members and developed by the Menu Planning Committee. This committee met once a month at a member's home to taste new recipes. They evaluated thousands of recipes and sent the ones they liked to the kitchen for testing. If favorably received by guests, the recipes were then added to the now 70-year collection and printed on a recipe card for sale.

Recipes have, of course, evolved over the years. Early recipes included creamy, rich foods. One recipe for Fresh Pea Soup required that the members shuck 20 pounds of peas and purée them by hand the way we did the vegetables for our babies.

Comfort food was in fashion for many years, and tasty casseroles containing rice or noodles were often featured. Creative Jell-o salads were also the order of the day.

As tastes changed toward lighter menus, entrée salads were added. Desserts became smaller and less rich.

Recipe cards were sold in boxes and individually. Soon, recipes from the Restaurant flooded the homes of the local and neighboring communities.

Tomato Herbed Fish Fillets

Yield: 8 servings

Even that rare person who dislikes fish will rave about this dish, topped with a creamy tomato sauce. Who would not savor each mouthful? This is a very reliable recipe that is a breeze to prepare.

1 (15-ounce) can diced tomatoes, drained
1/2 cup chopped green onions
2 teaspoons dried oregano leaves
2 teaspoons dried basil
Salt to taste
2 pounds firm white fish fillets, such as petrale sole or orange roughy,
   rinsed and dried
1/2 cup dry unseasoned bread crumbs
1/2 cup mayonnaise
1/2 cup sour cream
1 cup (4 ounces) shredded Cheddar cheese

Grease 8 individual ramekins or a large shallow casserole. Preheat the oven to 400 degrees. Combine the tomatoes, green onions, oregano and basil in a bowl. Let stand for 1 hour. Add salt to taste. Coat the fish fillets with the bread crumbs and arrange them in the prepared ramekins. Spoon 1/4 cup of the tomato mixture over each fillet. Combine the mayonnaise, sour cream and cheese. Spread about 1/4 cup over each fillet. Bake for 20 minutes. Garnish with chopped Italian parsley or sprigs of fresh basil.

Wine Note: *While an Italian orvieto or soave would be delicious,*
   you might think of a chilled rosé with this tomato-based sauce as well.

Shrimp Étouffée

Yield: 4 to 6 servings

The holy trinity—onions, celery, and green bell peppers—are the three most commonly used ingredients in Creole cooking. The Cajuns include garlic as well. Make this authentic Cajun recipe as mild or spicy as you desire by adjusting the amount of cayenne pepper used.

1/2 cup (1 stick) butter
1 cup finely chopped onion
2 celery ribs, cut into 1/4- to 1/3-inch pieces
1 cup cubed green bell pepper
1 1/2 teaspoons minced garlic
1 tablespoon paprika
1/8 teaspoon cayenne pepper, or to taste
2 tablespoons all-purpose flour
2 tablespoons tomato paste, or 1/4 cup
   tomato sauce
2 cups water
1 1/2 teaspoons salt, or to taste
1 1/2 pounds peeled and dried large shrimp
   (31- to 40-count)
Hot cooked rice

Wine Note: *The Cajun cuisine of the French immigrants to Louisiana is at its best when stunningly spicy. Champagne is an ideal accompaniment to an etouffee.*

Melt the butter in a large skillet over medium-low heat. Add the onion, celery, bell pepper and garlic. Sauté for 10 to 15 minutes or until tender. Reduce the heat to low. Stir in the paprika and cayenne pepper. Cook for 2 to 3 minutes longer. Sprinkle the flour over the vegetables. Cook for 1 to 2 minutes, stirring constantly. Stir in the tomato paste, water and salt. Bring to a boil and simmer, uncovered, for 12 to 15 minutes or until the sauce thickens, stirring occasionally. Reduce the heat to low and add the shrimp. Cook until the shrimp turn pink and are cooked through. Reduce the heat to the lowest possible temperature and allow the sauce to steep for 30 minutes to enhance the flavors. Serve over rice. Garnish with chopped green onion tops.

Mardi Gras Shrimp

Yield: 8 first-course servings or 4 entrée servings

Based on a New Orleans favorite, this quick and easy garlicky dish will earn raves. Serve it as a first course or as the entrée. Plenty of hot crisp French bread for dunking is a must. Don't forget the beer!

1/4 cup olive oil
1/4 cup (1/2 stick) butter
10 garlic cloves, crushed
4 bay leaves
1 1/2 teaspoons chopped fresh rosemary
1 1/2 teaspoons dried oregano leaves
1 1/2 teaspoons salt, or to taste
1 teaspoon red pepper flakes, or to taste
60 large prawns with tails on
    (31- to 40-count)
1/2 cup chardonnay or other dry white wine

Wine Note: *While a rich ale seems like the best choice for this spicy creation, a rosé Champagne might also work well.*

Heat the olive oil and butter in a large skillet over medium-low heat. Add the garlic. Cook for 5 minutes, stirring constantly and being careful not to let the garlic brown. Stir in the bay leaves, rosemary, oregano, salt and red pepper flakes. Increase the heat to medium and stir in the shrimp. Sauté the shrimp just until they turn pink. Stir in the wine and simmer for 5 minutes, being careful not to boil. Discard the bay leaves. Adjust the seasonings. Garnish with chopped fresh Italian parsley. Serve with French bread. Accompany entrée servings with a simple romaine salad topped with Parmesan cheese.

Fresco of Pottery Crafts

Seafood Florentine

Yield: 6 to 8 servings

This dish is sure to delight your fish-loving friends and family. Select your choice of seafood, arrange on a bed of spinach with mushrooms, and bake in a flavorful white sauce. Irresistible!

1 tablespoon butter
1 pound mushrooms, sliced
6 tablespoons butter
4 1/2 tablespoons all-purpose flour
3 cups milk, warmed
1 teaspoon salt
1/4 teaspoon pepper
1/4 teaspoon freshly grated nutmeg
3/4 cup finely chopped parsley
3 tablespoons dry sherry
2 (10-ounce) packages frozen chopped
    spinach, thawed and squeezed dry
1 1/2 pounds medium shrimp, peeled, rinsed
    and drained, or 6 (3- to 4-ounce) petrale
    sole, salmon or orange roughy fillets,
    topped with any combination of 1/2 cup
    small shrimp, 1/2 cup crab meat or
    1/2 cup bay scallops
1/2 cup (2 ounces) shredded Monterey
    Jack cheese
1/2 cup freshly grated Parmesan cheese
Paprika

Heat 1 tablespoon butter in a large skillet over medium heat. Add the mushrooms and sauté until the mushrooms are tender and the juices have evaporated. Melt 6 tablespoons butter in a large saucepan over medium heat. Whisk in the flour. Cook for 1 to 2 minutes, stirring constantly. Whisk in the milk and bring to a boil. Reduce the heat and simmer until the sauce thickens. Stir in the salt, pepper, nutmeg, parsley and sherry. Adjust the seasonings.

Grease a 9×13-inch baking dish or individual casseroles. Preheat the oven to 350 degrees. Combine the mushrooms, spinach and 1 1/4 cups of the sauce. Spread in the prepared baking dish. Arrange the shrimp over the mushroom mixture. Stir the Monterey Jack cheese into the remaining sauce in the saucepan and heat until the cheese is melted. Let the sauce stand until cool if the dish will not be baked immediately. Spoon evenly over the shrimp. Sprinkle with the Parmesan cheese and paprika. Bake for 30 minutes or until hot and bubbly.

Wine Note: *Chardonnay or a classic white burgundy is the ideal pairing.*

Shellfish Crêpes with Swiss Cheese-Wine Sauce

Yield: 12 servings

Prepare the separate components a day ahead and assemble just prior to baking. This recipe produces a delicate entrée perfect for a ladies' luncheon.

Swiss Cheese-Wine Sauce
1/3 cup dry vermouth or sherry
1 1/2 cups heavy cream
2 tablespoons cornstarch
2 tablespoons cold milk
1/4 teaspoon salt
Pepper to taste
1/3 cup shredded Swiss cheese, such
   as Gruyère

Filling
2 tablespoons butter
3 tablespoons minced shallots or
   green onions
1 1/2 cups shredded or chopped fresh or
   canned crab meat or raw shrimp or a
   mixture of shrimp and bay scallops
1/4 cup dry vermouth or sherry
1/4 teaspoon Tabasco sauce
Salt and pepper to taste

Assembly
12 crêpes (see Basic Crêpe recipe, page 140)
1/3 cup shredded Swiss cheese, such
   as Gruyère
2 tablespoons butter

Wine Note: The perfect wine for a ladies' luncheon would be a delicate and dry German trocken or halbtrocken Riesling.

For the wine sauce, boil the vermouth in a nonstick skillet until reduced to about 1 tablespoon. Remove the skillet from the heat and add the cream. Combine the cornstarch and milk in a small dish and stir until the cornstarch is dissolved. Add the cornstarch mixture, salt and pepper to the cream mixture. Increase the heat and simmer for 2 minutes or until the sauce thickens, stirring constantly. Add the cheese and stir until melted.

For the filling, melt the butter in a nonstick skillet over medium-high heat. Add the shallots. Sauté until translucent. Add the shellfish and sauté for 1 minute. Stir in the vermouth, Tabasco sauce, salt and pepper. Simmer until most of the liquid has evaporated. Stir in enough of the wine sauce to bind the mixture together. Spoon into a medium bowl. Chill, covered, until ready to assemble the crêpes.

To assemble, grease a large baking dish. Preheat the oven to 350 degrees. Spoon 1 heaping tablespoon of the seafood filling over the lower third of each crêpe. Roll the crêpes to enclose the filling and place in the prepared baking dish seam side down. Spoon the remaining wine sauce over the crêpes. Sprinkle with the cheese and dot with the butter. Chill the crêpes, covered, if they are not to be baked immediately. Let stand at room temperature for 15 to 20 minutes. Bake for 15 to 20 minutes or until hot and bubbly and the cheese is lightly browned.

Ratatouille Lasagna

Yield: 8 servings

An assortment of chunky vegetables and Italian spices flavors this unique lasagna. It will surely satisfy vegetarians and meat-lovers alike.

Sauce
1/4 cup olive oil
4 ounces mushrooms, sliced
1/2 cup chopped onion
2 garlic cloves, minced
8 ounces small zucchini
1/2 cup shredded carrots
1 pound unpeeled eggplant, cut into
   1/2-inch cubes
1 (14-ounce) can diced Italian-style
   tomatoes
1 (8-ounce) can tomato sauce
1/2 cup dry red wine
1 1/2 tablespoons Italian seasoning
1/4 cup chopped Italian parsley
2 teaspoons salt
1/4 teaspoon red pepper flakes
1/4 teaspoon black pepper

Spinach Filling
1 (10-ounce) package frozen chopped
   spinach, thawed and squeezed dry
2 cups cottage cheese

Assembly
8 ounces lasagna noodles, cooked
2 cups (8 ounces) shredded mozzarella
   cheese
1 1/2 cups grated Parmesan cheese

Wine Note: *This vegetarian offering could pair equally well with a chardonnay or a chilled pinot noir.*

For the sauce, heat the olive oil in a large skillet. Add the mushrooms, onion and garlic and sauté until tender. Slice the zucchini in half lengthwise and cut into 1/4-inch lengths. Add with the carrots and eggplant to the skillet. Sauté for 15 minutes, stirring frequently. Stir in the tomatoes, tomato sauce, red wine, Italian seasoning, parsley, salt, red pepper flakes and black pepper. Bring to a boil. Reduce the heat and simmer, covered, for 30 minutes. Cook, uncovered, for 15 minutes longer, or until the sauce thickens.

For the filling, combine the spinach and cottage cheese in a food processor fitted with a steel blade. Process until smooth.

To assemble, grease a 9×13-inch baking dish. Preheat the oven to 350 degrees. Spread 1/4 of the sauce in the prepared baking dish. Layer 1/3 of the lasagna noodles, 1/3 of the spinach filling, 1/3 of the mozzarella cheese and 1/4 of the Parmesan cheese over the sauce. Repeat these layers twice more, ending with the Parmesan cheese. Bake, covered, for 45 minutes or until hot and bubbly. Let stand for 5 minutes before serving.

Tortellini Primavera

Yield: 4 entrée servings or 8 to
10 buffet servings

*A creamy white sauce filled with fresh vegetables
combines with cheese-filled pasta to adorn a
buffet table or to spoon onto dinner plates right
in the kitchen.*

2 tablespoons olive oil
3/4 cup chopped onion
1/2 cup julienned carrots
1/4 cup julienned red bell pepper
1 large garlic clove, minced
1 cup sliced mushrooms
1/2 cup thinly sliced small zucchini
6 ounces fresh spinach leaves, chopped
8 ounces cream cheese, softened
1/2 cup milk
1/3 cup grated Parmesan cheese
1/4 cup chopped fresh basil
1 teaspoon Italian seasoning
1/4 teaspoon salt, or to taste
1/8 teaspoon pepper, or to taste
1/2 cup chopped prosciutto (optional)
1 (8- to 9-ounce) package cheese-filled
    tortellini

Heat the olive oil in a large skillet. Add the
onion, carrots, bell pepper and garlic and sauté until
tender. Add the mushrooms, zucchini and spinach.
Sauté until the spinach wilts. Heat the cream cheese
and milk in a large saucepan, stirring until smooth.
Stir in the sautéed vegetables, Parmesan cheese,
basil, Italian seasoning, salt, pepper and prosciutto.
Cook until the sauce is bubbly and thick enough
to coat the tortellini, stirring constantly and adding
milk if necessary to thin. Adjust the seasonings.
Cook the tortellini using the package directions;
drain. Combine the tortellini and sauce in a large
serving bowl and toss to combine. Garnish with
chopped seeded tomatoes and sprigs of fresh basil.

Wine Note: *Any of the Italian white wines, such as pinot
grigio or orvieto, would be delicious, but it might be
even better to experiment with one of the rare Italian
chardonnays.*

Creamy Macaroni and Cheese

Yield: 8 servings

This American classic, served once a year at the Restaurant to finicky kids attending the Bunny Days event, will never go out of style.

1 (8-ounce) package elbow macaroni
1/4 cup (1/2 stick) butter
1/4 cup all-purpose flour
1/2 teaspoon salt
1/2 teaspoon pepper
2 cups milk, heated
8 ounces shredded Cheddar cheese
1/2 cup butter-flavored cracker crumbs, or
    1 cup fresh bread crumbs
1/4 cup grated Parmesan cheese
3 tablespoons butter, melted

Wine Note: *Macaroni and cheese calls for a Bordeaux-style wine, such as cabernet sauvignon or merlot.*

Grease a 2 1/2-quart casserole. Preheat the oven to 350 degrees. Cook the macaroni until al dente using the package directions; rinse under cold water and drain. Melt 1/4 cup butter in a large saucepan over medium heat. Stir in the flour, salt and pepper. Cook for 1 to 2 minutes, stirring constantly. Whisk in the milk and bring to a boil. Cook until the sauce has thickened, stirring constantly. Lower the heat and add the Cheddar cheese; stir until melted. Add the macaroni and mix well. Pour into the prepared casserole. Combine the cracker crumbs, Parmesan cheese and 3 tablespoons melted butter in a bowl and mix well. Sprinkle over the casserole. Bake, uncovered, for 25 to 30 minutes or until heated through and bubbly. Garnish with finely chopped fresh parsley.

Zucchini Cheese Frittata

Yield: 6 servings

Vegetarians, take note of this crustless cheese pie. Try it topped with salsa or your favorite tomato-based spaghetti sauce. A green salad and glass of wine could round out the meal.

5 eggs
4 cups grated unpeeled zucchini
   (about 4 medium zucchini)
2 cups (8 ounces) shredded mozzarella cheese
1/2 cup finely chopped onion
1/2 cup grated Parmesan cheese
1/4 cup olive oil
1/2 cup all-purpose flour
1/4 teaspoon baking powder
1/2 teaspoon Italian seasoning
1/2 teaspoon garlic salt
1/4 teaspoon black pepper

Butter a 10-inch pie plate or quiche pan. Preheat the oven to 350 degrees. Beat the eggs until foamy in a large bowl. Add the zucchini, mozzarella cheese, onion, Parmesan cheese, olive oil, flour, baking powder, Italian seasoning, garlic salt and pepper and mix well. Pour into the prepared pie plate. Bake for 45 minutes or until slightly puffed in the middle and golden. Let stand for 10 minutes before slicing. Serve hot or at room temperature. Reheat slices of the cold leftover frittata at 350 degrees for about 20 minutes.

Wine Note: *A rich wine, such as zinfandel or syrah, would be perfect with this cheesy dish.*

Lunch on the Terrace

When the Restaurant was still quite young, the volunteers served lunch on an open terrace by the Blue Garden, or the Garden of Delight. Wisteria hung on trellises over the terrace, and the garden was lush with wild lilac, crabapples, and pink magnolia.

There was a constant demand for seating on the terrace. People loved it so much they didn't mind wisteria petals and caterpillars falling into their lunch!

In later years, the terrace was enclosed with glass to provide year-round seating, to keep the luncheon plates free of bugs and to continue offering the spectacular view. Guests were then able to enjoy lunch without the falling caterpillars.

We will never forget the early days, however, when eating around the caterpillars was actually considered the essence of politeness!

Rose Path

Chocolate Pecan Pie

Yield: 8 servings

Based on a holiday tradition, but raised to another level with the addition of chocolate plus a smidgen of your favorite alcohol, this pie is a breeze to make.

> 1 cup coarsely chopped pecans
> 1 cup (6 ounces) semisweet chocolate chips
> 1 baked (9-inch) pie shell
>   (we recommend Cream Cheese Crust, page 29)
> 3 eggs
> 1/2 cup light corn syrup
> 1/2 cup sugar
> 1 tablespoon bourbon, rum or brandy
> 1/4 cup (1/2 stick) butter, melted and cooled

Preheat the oven to 350 degrees. Sprinkle the pecans and chocolate chips evenly over the pie shell. Beat the eggs until foamy in a bowl. Add the corn syrup, sugar and bourbon and mix well. Stir in the butter. Pour into the pie shell, spreading evenly. Bake for 1 hour or until firm. Serve warm or at room temperature with Eggnog Sauce (page 172), whipped cream, vanilla ice cream or frozen yogurt.

Niche in the Dining Room

Java Pie

Yield: 6 to 8 servings

A one-time favorite at the Restaurant, this recipe was removed from the menu because of the salmonella scare from raw eggs. We now use either pasteurized eggs or powdered egg whites to once again enjoy this wonderful pie. Refrigerate it overnight.

Macaroon Crumb Crust
1^1/2 cups finely ground coconut macaroon crumbs
(about 15 small cookies)
3 tablespoons unsalted butter, softened
^{1}/4 cup finely chopped toasted slivered almonds
1 ounce semisweet chocolate, grated

Filling
^{1}/2 cup (1 stick) butter, softened
^{1}/2 cup confectioners' sugar
1 ounce unsweetened chocolate, melted and cooled slightly
2 teaspoons instant coffee
2 whole pasteurized eggs, or 2 tablespoons plus 2 teaspoons
powdered egg whites, reconstituted

Whipped Cream Topping
1 cup chilled heavy whipping cream
1 teaspoon instant coffee
2 tablespoons confectioners' sugar
Grated chocolate

For the crust, combine the macaroon crumbs and butter in a food processor fitted with a steel blade and process until well blended. Add the almonds and chocolate and process until well combined. Press the crumb mixture evenly into a 9-inch pie plate. Chill.

For the filling, cream the butter and confectioners' sugar in a mixing bowl for 4 minutes. Beat in the chocolate and coffee. Add the eggs 1 at a time and beat at high speed for 5 minutes per egg or until the batter quadruples in size. Follow the procedure in the sidebar to substitute powdered egg whites. Pour the filling into the cooled crumb crust. Chill, covered, for 8 hours.

For the whipped cream topping, beat the whipping cream with the coffee and confectioners' sugar in a mixing bowl until stiff peaks form. Spread over the filling. Sprinkle grated chocolate over the top. Chill until serving time.

Raw Egg Safety for Java Pie

*When making Java Pie, use pasteurized eggs or powdered egg whites. Avoid using all other raw eggs due to the risk of salmonella. Look for pasteurized eggs at Safeway and other name-brand grocers. If unavailable, substitute powdered egg whites found at upscale markets, such as Draeger's or Whole Foods. Do **not** substitute Egg Beaters in this recipe.*

To make Java Pie with pasteurized eggs, simply use 2 whole pasteurized eggs (including the yolks) as specified in the recipe.

To make Java Pie using powdered egg whites, combine the butter, sugar, chocolate, and coffee as directed in the recipe. Transfer mixture to another large bowl.

Wash the original mixing bowl and attach the whisk attachment. Add 2 tablespoons plus 2 teaspoons powdered egg white to the mixing bowl. Stir in ^{1}/2 cup warm water and let it stand for a few minutes. Beat the egg white-water mixture at a high speed, scraping down the bowl as needed, until stiff peaks form. Fold ^{1}/3 of the egg whites into the chocolate-coffee mixture until well incorporated. Gently fold in the remaining egg whites until just blended. Pour into the cooled shell and refrigerate overnight. Top with whipped cream topping and garnish with chocolate in accordance with recipe directions.

160

Applesauce Spice Cake with Caramel Frosting

Yield: 12 to 16 servings

Instant coffee teams up with a variety of spices to produce this decades-old standby served in the Restaurant since 1977. It's guaranteed to become a favorite in your home as well.

Cake

2 cups sugar
1 cup vegetable oil
2 eggs
2 cups applesauce
2 cups all-purpose flour
2 teaspoons baking soda
2 teaspoons cinnamon

1 teaspoon ground cloves
1 teaspoon nutmeg
1 teaspoon salt
2 teaspoons instant coffee powder
1 cup raisins
1$^{1}/_{2}$ cups chopped toasted walnuts
  or pecans

Caramel Frosting

$^{1}/_{2}$ cup (1 stick) butter
1 cup packed brown sugar
$^{1}/_{4}$ cup half-and-half

2 cups sifted confectioners' sugar
1 teaspoon vanilla extract

For the cake, grease a 9×13-inch cake pan; dust with flour. Preheat the oven to 350 degrees. Beat the sugar and oil in a large bowl. Add the eggs and applesauce and beat until smooth. Sift the flour, baking soda, cinnamon, cloves, nutmeg, salt and instant coffee powder into a bowl. Add to the sugar mixture and mix well. Stir in the raisins and 1 cup of the walnuts. Pour into the prepared pan. Bake for 45 to 50 minutes or until the cake tests done. Let stand until cool. Spread the frosting over the top of the cake. Sprinkle with the remaining $^{1}/_{2}$ cup walnuts.

For the frosting, combine the butter, brown sugar and half-and-half in a saucepan over medium-high heat. Bring to a boil, stirring constantly. Boil for 2 minutes, stirring constantly. Add the confectioners' sugar and beat until creamy. Stir in the vanilla.

Tropical Carrot Cake with Orange Cream Cheese Frosting

Yield: 12 to 16 servings

All our testers judged this carrot cake recipe as the best one they could find. It definitely deserves their "thumbs-up" reviews. The cake freezes beautifully either before or after frosting.

Cake

2 cups all-purpose flour
2 teaspoons baking soda
2 teaspoons cinnamon
1/8 teaspoon nutmeg
1/2 teaspoon salt
3 eggs
3/4 cup vegetable oil
3/4 cup buttermilk

3/4 cup granulated sugar
1 cup packed light brown sugar
2 teaspoons vanilla extract
1 (8-ounce) can crushed pineapple, drained
2 cup grated carrots (4 medium carrots)
1 cup flaked coconut
1 cup chopped walnuts or pecans
1 teaspoon grated orange zest

Buttermilk Glaze

1/4 cup (1/2 stick) butter
1/2 cup sugar
1/4 cup buttermilk

1/4 teaspoon baking soda
1 1/2 teaspoons light corn syrup
1/2 teaspoon vanilla extract

Orange Cream Cheese Frosting

8 ounces cream cheese, softened
1/2 cup (1 stick) unsalted butter, softened
2 cups confectioners' sugar

1 teaspoon vanilla extract
1 teaspoon orange juice
2 teaspoons grated orange zest

For the cake, butter a 9×13-inch cake pan. Preheat the oven to 325 degrees. Combine the flour, baking soda, cinnamon, nutmeg and salt in a bowl. Beat the eggs in a large bowl until foamy. Add the oil, buttermilk, granulated sugar, brown sugar and vanilla and mix well. Add the flour mixture and mix well. Stir in the pineapple, carrots, coconut, walnuts and 1 teaspoon orange zest. Pour into the prepared pan. Bake for 40 minutes or until the cake tests done. Let stand until warm. Top the warm cake with Buttermilk Glaze. Let stand until cool. Spread Orange Cream Cheese Frosting over the top. Garnish with orange zest.

For the glaze, combine the butter, sugar, buttermilk, baking soda, corn syrup and vanilla in a saucepan and bring to a boil. Boil for 1 minute.

For the frosting, beat the cream cheese and butter together in a bowl. Add the confectioners' sugar, vanilla, orange juice and orange zest. Beat until the frosting is thick and smooth. Thin with an additional teaspoon of orange juice if necessary.

Lemon Lovers' Delight

Yield: 12 to 16 servings

The name speaks for itself! Luscious layers of lemon cake are filled with lemon curd and topped with lemon-flavored whipped cream.

1 cup (2 sticks) butter, softened
1 1/2 cups sugar
3 eggs, beaten
1 cup sour cream
3 tablespoons grated lemon zest
2 tablespoons fresh lemon juice
1 teaspoon vanilla extract
2 1/2 cups all-purpose flour
1 teaspoon baking powder
1 teaspoon baking soda
1/4 teaspoon salt
1 cup lemon curd, preferably homemade (see sidebar)
1 cup heavy whipping cream
Sliced strawberries
Confectioners' sugar

Line the bottom of a 9×13-inch cake pan with parchment paper. Butter the paper and the sides of the pan. Preheat the oven to 350 degrees. Cream the butter and sugar in a large mixing bowl until light and fluffy. Add the eggs, sour cream, lemon zest, lemon juice and vanilla and mix well. Combine the flour, baking powder, baking soda and salt in a bowl. Add to the creamed mixture a little at a time, mixing well after each addition. Pour into the prepared pan. Bake for 55 to 60 minutes or until the center springs back to the touch and the cake tests done. Cool completely in the pan.

Remove the cake from the pan and split in half horizontally with a bread knife. Remove 2 tablespoons of the lemon curd and reserve. Spread the remaining lemon curd evenly over 1 layer. Cover with the other layer. Chill, tightly covered, until serving time. Whip the cream in a mixing bowl until soft peaks form. Fold the reserved lemon curd gently into the cream. Frost the cake with the cream. Garnish with sliced strawberries arranged in a pinwheel in the middle of the cake or shingle-fashion over the entire top of the cake. Chill until serving time. Sprinkle with confectioners' sugar just before serving.

Lemon Curd

Yield: 1 cup

Melt 1/4 cup unsalted butter in the top of a double boiler set over simmering water. Stir in 1/4 cup lemon juice, 1 teaspoon lemon zest, 3/4 cup sugar and 1/8 teaspoon salt. Beat 1/2 cup egg yolks (from 6 to 7 eggs) into butter mixture, whisking continuously until curd becomes thick and smooth, about 20 minutes. Pour curd into a small bowl. Place plastic wrap directly on the surface to prevent a skin from forming. Store in the refrigerator for up to 6 weeks. Flavor is best after 2 days rest.

Spread on scones, biscuits, muffins, or toast. Also use as a filling for tarts, cream puffs, or cake layers.

Mandelbrot

Yield: 60 (1/2-inch-thick) bars or 48 (3/4-inch-thick) bars

This prize-winning recipe—over one hundred years old—
requires that you blend the dough by hand. These fine
Jewish biscotti beg you to savor each blissful bite.

1 cup sugar
3/4 cup vegetable oil
3 eggs
2 3/4 cups all-purpose flour
1 teaspoon baking powder
1 teaspoon cinnamon
1/4 teaspoon salt
1 cup coarsely chopped slivered almonds or walnuts

Grease 2 cookie sheets. Combine the sugar and oil in a large bowl and mix well by hand. Add the eggs 1 at a time, mixing well after each addition. Combine the flour, baking powder, cinnamon and salt in a small bowl. Add to the egg mixture 1/3 at a time, mixing well after each addition. Stir in the almonds. The dough will be sticky, but do not add more flour. Chill for 30 to 60 minutes. Preheat the oven to 350 degrees. Divide the dough into 4 equal portions. Shape each into a 1/2×2-inch loaf. Place 2 loaves 4 inches apart on each cookie sheet. Bake for 30 minutes. Cut the loaves into 1/2-inch or 3/4-inch slices. Place the slices close together on the cookie sheets cut side down. Bake for 10 to 12 minutes longer or until lightly browned. Turn off the heat and let the cookies stand in the oven for 30 minutes. Remove to a wire rack to cool completely. Store in an airtight container.

Polka Dot Cookies

Yield: 5 dozen cookies

These zesty lemon confections are dotted with tiny chocolate morsels. Make the dough ahead, refrigerate for two hours or overnight, and then slice and bake.

Cookies
3/4 cup (1¹/2 sticks) butter, softened
1 cup sugar
1 egg
Grated zest of 1 lemon
1 tablespoon fresh lemon juice
2 cups all-purpose flour
1 teaspoon baking powder
1 cup (6 ounces) miniature semisweet chocolate chips

Lemon Glaze
1 cup confectioners' sugar
Juice of ¹/2 lemon
1 tablespoon butter, softened

For the cookies, cream the butter and sugar in a mixing bowl until light and fluffy. Add the egg, lemon zest and lemon juice and mix well. Combine the flour and baking powder and add to the creamed mixture. Stir in the chocolate chips. Divide the dough into 2 equal portions. Shape each into a roll 2 inches in diameter. Chill, tightly wrapped, in the refrigerator for 2 to 8 hours. Preheat the oven to 350 degrees. Cut the rolls ¹/4-inch slices. Bake on ungreased cookie sheets for 10 to 12 minutes. Cool slightly before removing f

For the lemon glaze, combine the confectioners' sugar, lemon juice and butter in a small bo. well. Add more confectioners' sugar or lemon juice to reach a spreading consistency. Spread over th

Swedish Ginger Cookies

Yield: about 70 cookies

Just the right amount of orange zest and spice creates one of the best cutout cookies we could find. Let the kids help cut into whatever shape fits the occasion.

1 cup (2 sticks) butter, softened
1 1/2 cups sugar
1 tablespoon light corn syrup
1 tablespoon molasses
2 teaspoons baking soda
1 egg
3 3/4 cups all-purpose flour
2 teaspoons cinnamon
1 teaspoon ginger
1 teaspoon ground cloves
1/4 teaspoon nutmeg
Grated zest of 1 orange
2 tablespoons orange juice

Grease cookie sheets. Preheat the oven to 350 degrees. Cream the butter and sugar in a mixing bowl until light and fluffy. Add the corn syrup, molasses, baking soda and egg and mix well. Sift the flour, cinnamon, ginger, cloves and nutmeg together and add to the creamed mixture. Stir in the orange zest and orange juice. Shape the dough into a ball. Chill until firm enough to roll. Roll 1/8 inch thick on a floured surface. Cut into desired shapes and place on the prepared cookie sheets. Bake for 8 to 10 minutes. Cool on a wire rack. Store in an airtight container.

Chocolate Mint Bars

Yield: 36 (1×2-inch) bars or 80 (1×1-inch) bars

Peppermint flavor, an unrivaled companion for chocolate, enlivens the taste buds after a delicious meal.

Chocolate Mint Bars

2 ounces unsweetened chocolate
$1/2$ cup (1 stick) butter
2 eggs, beaten
1 cup sugar

1 teaspoon salt
$1/4$ teaspoon peppermint extract
1 teaspoon vanilla extract
$1/2$ cup all-purpose flour

Peppermint Frosting

$1^1/2$ cups confectioners' sugar
3 tablespoons cream

2 tablespoons butter, softened
$1/2$ teaspoon peppermint extract

Chocolate Glaze

2 ounces semisweet chocolate

2 tablespoons butter

For the bars, line a 9×9-inch baking pan with parchment paper; grease the paper and the sides of the pan. Preheat the oven to 350 degrees. Melt the chocolate and butter in a small saucepan over low heat. Let cool slightly. Combine the eggs, sugar, salt, peppermint extract and vanilla in a mixing bowl and mix well. Stir in the flour. Add the chocolate mixture and blend well. Pour into the prepared pan. Bake for 20 to 25 minutes or until the edges begin to pull away from the pan. Let stand until cool.

For the frosting, cream the confectioners' sugar, cream, butter and peppermint extract in a mixing bowl until light and fluffy. Spread over the cooled cake.

For the glaze, melt the chocolate and butter in a small saucepan over low heat, stirring until smooth. Drizzle over the frosted layer. Chill until the glaze is set. Cut into bars.

Heavenly Squares

Yield: 117 (1-inch) pieces

These squares are sometimes referred to as "food for the gods" because, as the name implies, they are heavenly.

Squares

1/2 cup (1 stick) butter, softened
1 cup all-purpose flour
1 tablespoon granulated sugar
2 eggs
1 cup packed brown sugar
1 tablespoon all-purpose flour
1 teaspoon vanilla extract
1 cup finely chopped walnuts
1/2 cup flaked coconut

Lemon Glaze

1 cup confectioners' sugar
2 teaspoons lemon juice, or 1 teaspoon vanilla extract
Confectioners' sugar

For the squares, grease a 9×13-inch baking pan. Preheat the oven to 350 degrees. Combine the butter, 1 cup flour and the granulated sugar in a bowl and mix well. Press onto the bottom of the prepared baking pan. Bake for 15 minutes or until lightly browned. Let stand until cool. Reduce the oven temperature to 275 degrees. Beat the eggs in a medium bowl until fluffy. Add the brown sugar, 1 tablespoon flour and vanilla and mix well. Fold in the walnuts and coconut. Pour evenly over the crust. Bake for 20 minutes or until set.

For the glaze, combine the confectioners' sugar and lemon juice in a small bowl and mix well. Add enough water to make a thin glaze. Drizzle the glaze over the baked layer as soon as it comes from the oven. Let cool. Cut into 1-inch squares and serve in small colored cupcake liners, if desired. Shake confectioners' sugar over the squares before serving.

Almond Shortbread Tarts

Yield: 70 to 80 miniature tarts

These tarts have the taste of an amaretto cookie. When heated in the microwave for fifteen seconds, they become soft and chewy. Make them ahead and freeze for a great holiday gift.

Almond Filling
14 ounces almond paste, crumbled
1¹/2 tablespoons fresh lemon juice
1 egg
1 cup sugar

Shortbread
1 cup (2 sticks) unsalted butter, softened
1 cup sugar
1 egg
¹/2 teaspoon grated lemon zest
2 cups all-purpose flour
¹/8 teaspoon salt

Tarts
Lemon juice
1¹/2 tablespoons finely chopped slivered almonds
Confectioners' sugar

For the filling, combine the almond paste, lemon juice and egg in a bowl and mix well. Stir in the sugar a little at a time. Chill, covered, in the refrigerator.

For the shortbread, cream the butter and sugar in a large mixing bowl until light and fluffy. Beat in the egg and lemon zest. Combine the flour and salt and add to the creamed mixture, mixing until smooth. Turn the dough out onto a piece of plastic wrap; top with another piece of plastic wrap. Mold and flatten the dough to a ³/4-inch thickness. Chill, tightly wrapped in the plastic wrap, for at least 30 minutes.

For the tarts, grease miniature muffin cups. Preheat the oven to 325 degrees. Scoop pieces of the dough with the large end of a melon baller. Shape into balls and press each ball into the bottom and up the side of a prepared muffin cup. Chill the dough briefly if it becomes too sticky while forming the tarts. Spoon about 1 teaspoon of the filling into each tart. Press the filling gently into the bottom of the tart, using a finger dipped in lemon juice. Sprinkle a few of the chopped almonds over the filling. Bake for 20 to 25 minutes or until golden. Cool for 10 minutes. Remove the tarts from the muffin cups, using the tip of a paring knife to loosen them. Cool completely on a wire rack. Sprinkle confectioners' sugar over the tarts. Store in the freezer, if desired.

Buon Giorno, Signore

One warm summer Friday a group of very dejected-looking Italian ladies arrived at the Restaurant, herded in by a rather militant non-Italian-speaking tour guide. It was obvious that the ladies, who were wives of Italian executives attending a convention in San Francisco, had been talked AT all morning and were exhausted by their attempts to translate every spoken word.

Fortunately, one of our Friday servers had been a high fashion model working for Ungaro in Milan, Italy. We dispatched her to the table to explain the luncheon choices in her flawless Italian. "Buon giorno, Signore," she began, "Welcome to Allied Arts!" The executives' spouses were enchanted. Like wilted flowers returned to cold water, their heads came up and they began to speak animatedly among themselves.

A small détente perhaps, but proof of our being a "full-service restaurant."

Chocolate Chip Rum Torte with Eggnog Sauce

Yield: 12 servings

Want to impress that very special guest? Here's the answer. Serve this rich moist treat as the grand finale at your next dinner party. We think it's the best thing that ever happened to chocolate.

Torte

1 1/2 cups finely crushed graham cracker crumbs
1 1/4 cups finely chopped pecans
1/2 cup packed brown sugar
2 teaspoons baking powder
3/4 cup semisweet chocolate chips
5 egg whites, at room temperature (reserve 2 egg yolks for Eggnog Sauce)
1 cup granulated sugar
1/4 teaspoon salt
2 teaspoons rum, or 1/2 teaspoon rum extract

Chocolate Glaze

1/2 cup whipping cream
1/2 teaspoon instant coffee
1 cup (6 ounces) semisweet chocolate chips
1/2 teaspoon vanilla extract

Eggnog Sauce

2 egg yolks
1/2 cup sugar
1 tablespoon all-purpose flour
2 tablespoons cream
4 tablespoons butter
2 tablespoons rum, or 1/2 teaspoon rum extract
1/2 teaspoon vanilla extract
4 ounces whipped topping, or 1/2 cup whipping cream, whipped

For the torte, grease and flour a 10-inch springform pan or cake pan lined with parchment paper. Preheat the oven to 350 degrees. Combine the graham cracker crumbs, pecans, brown sugar and baking powder in a bowl and mix well. Stir in the chocolate chips. Beat the egg whites in a mixing bowl until soft peaks form. Add the granulated sugar and salt gradually, beating until stiff peaks form. Fold in the rum. Fold the graham cracker mixture gently into the egg whites. Pour into the prepared pan. Bake for 35 minutes. Let stand until cool. Run a sharp knife around the cake and remove the side of the springform pan.

For the chocolate glaze, combine the cream and instant coffee in a small saucepan and bring to a simmer. Add the chocolate chips and stir until melted. Stir in the vanilla. Remove from the heat and let cool slightly. Pour over the cooled torte, letting it spill over the side. Slice the torte with a serrated knife. Serve with Eggnog Sauce.

For the sauce, measure all the ingredients before beginning. Beat the egg yolks and sugar in a heavy saucepan over low heat until the sugar has dissolved and the mixture is thick and pale yellow. Stir in the flour and cream. Add the butter 1 tablespoon at a time, stirring constantly for 10 minutes or until the butter melts and the sauce thickens. Remove from the heat and stir in the rum and vanilla. Set the saucepan in ice water and stir the sauce for 10 minutes or until it cools. Fold in the whipped topping. Chill until serving time. Store for up to 1 week. Serve on any dessert, including fresh fruit, as a substitute for whipped cream.

Lemon Cheesecake

Yield: 10 to 12 servings

We think this rich and creamy cake with a hint of lemon may be the queen of cheesecakes. It requires refrigeration overnight before serving.

3/4 cup finely chopped toasted almonds
3 tablespoons confectioners' sugar
3/4 cup vanilla wafer crumbs
5 tablespoons unsalted butter, melted
24 ounces cream cheese, cut into 1-inch chunks, softened
1 cup sugar
1/4 cup fresh lemon juice
1 tablespoon grated lemon zest
3 eggs, at room temperature

Butter the bottom and side of a 9-inch springform pan. Preheat the oven to 325 degrees. Combine the almonds, confectioners' sugar and vanilla wafer crumbs in a food processor and process until well mixed. Add the butter and process until crumbly. Press the crumbs into the bottom and up the side of the prepared pan. Chill the crust.

Beat the cream cheese in the large bowl of a heavy-duty mixer fitted with a flat beater for 1 minute or until fluffy. Add the sugar a little at a time, beating well after each addition. Beat in the lemon juice and lemon zest. Add the eggs and beat at medium speed for 1 minute or just until incorporated. Pour into the crust and smooth the surface. Set the pan on the middle rack of the preheated oven. Set a pan of boiling water beside the cheesecake pan. Bake for 1 hour or until the center is just set and jiggles slightly when the pan is shaken and the top appears glossy. The temperature will measure 145 to 150 degrees on an instant-read thermometer. Remove to a wire rack. Loosen the cake with the tip of a paring knife and remove the side of the pan. Cool at room temperature for at least 3 hours. Chill, tightly wrapped, for 8 hours.

Let the cheesecake stand at room temperature for 30 minutes before serving. Slice and garnish individual servings with small lemon wedges. Garnish the sides with sprigs of fresh mint. Place the cheesecake, unwrapped, in the freezer until frozen and then wrap tightly in plastic wrap and heavy-duty foil. Store in the freezer for up to 1 month. Defrost in the refrigerator for 8 hours.

Mini-Lemon Cheesecake Bites

To convert Lemon Cheesecake into individual bite-size servings, assemble crust and filling ingredients as directed. Preheat oven to 325 degrees. Spray mini-muffin tins with butter spray. Press 1 teaspoon crust mixture into bottom of each cup. Fill with 1 tablespoon filling. Set a pan of hot water in oven beside the mini-muffin tin. Bake about 15 minutes or until center registers between 145 and 150 degrees on an instant-read thermometer. Remove to a rack. Cool in pan for at least 1 hour. Decorate tops with fresh fruit, lemon curd, chopped nuts, grated chocolate, and so forth. If desired, freeze before decorating tops.

Orange Cheesecake Flan

Yield: 8 servings

This is a cross between two popular desserts. Allow five or more hours for chilling.

Orange Glaze
$1/2$ cup sugar
3 tablespoons orange marmalade
Juice of $1/2$ orange

Cheesecake Flan
8 ounces cream cheese, softened
$1/2$ cup sugar
1 teaspoon vanilla extract
1 tablespoon grated orange zest
6 eggs, at room temprature
2 cups milk, at room temperature
Fresh orange segments

For the glaze, butter a 9-inch round baking pan. Combine the sugar, orange marmalade and orange juice in a small saucepan over medium heat. Bring to a boil and simmer for 5 to 6 minutes or until the mixture thickens slightly, stirring occasionally. Pour $1/2$ of the glaze into the prepared cake pan, tilting to coat the bottom evenly. Chill until the glaze hardens. Reserve the remaining glaze for the garnish.

For the flan, preheat the oven to 350 degrees. Beat the cream cheese in the large bowl of an electric mixer until light and fluffy. Beat in the sugar, vanilla and orange zest. Add the eggs 1 at a time, beating at medium speed after each addition until smooth. Beat in the milk at very low speed. Pour the cream cheese mixture over the orange glaze in the pan. Place the pan in a larger baking pan. Add water to the larger pan to a depth of 1 inch. Bake for 1 hour and 10 minutes or until the center is set and a knife inserted in the center comes out clean. Cool on a wire rack. Chill for at least 5 hours. Loosen the custard from the pan edge with a knife, and invert onto a rimmed serving dish. Reheat the reserved orange glaze. Dip orange segments in the glaze and arrange in a circle over the middle of the cake.

Crème Parisienne with Raspberry Sauce

Yield: 10 servings

Here is a treat for the eyes as well as the taste buds. You will think you've died and gone to heaven after just one taste of this sophisticated, creamy, flavorful dessert. You may also serve the dessert with any of your other favorite sauces. It requires four hours of refrigeration before serving.

Raspberry Sauce
    1 (10- or 12-ounce) package frozen sweetened raspberries, thawed
    1/3 cup seedless raspberry preserves
    1 tablespoon fresh lemon juice or orange liqueur

Crème Parisienne
    1 envelope unflavored gelatin
    1/4 cup cold water
    12 ounces cream cheese, cut into pieces
    1 cup heavy whipping cream
    2/3 cup sugar
    1 3/4 cups sour cream
    3/4 teaspoon vanilla extract
    30 fresh raspberries (optional)

For the sauce, press the raspberries through a sieve into a bowl, discarding the seeds. Add the preserves and lemon juice to the purée and mix well. Chill, covered, until serving time.

For the crème, double-coat ten 4-ounce molds (not Tupperware) with nonstick cooking spray. Soften the gelatin in the water. Heat the cream cheese, cream and sugar in the top of a double boiler over simmering water. Cook until smooth, stirring constantly with a whisk. Stir in the softened gelatin. Cook until the gelatin completely dissolves, stirring constantly. Remove from the heat and stir in the sour cream and vanilla. Pour into the prepared molds. Chill until firm. Let stand at room temperature for 20 to 30 minutes before serving. Dip the molds in hot water for a few seconds to loosen. Run a knife around the side of the mold if necessary. Unmold onto individual dessert plates. Spoon Raspberry Sauce around each mold. Place 3 raspberries in the sauce around each dessert. Garnish with fresh mint sprigs.

Almond Coconut Parfait

Yield: 8 servings

For coconut lovers, this dessert tastes just like a very popular candy bar.
Guess which one! The crust and custard may be made the day before assembly.
It requires refrigeration to set the custard before serving.

Coconut Crust
2 ounces unsweetened chocolate
2 tablespoons butter
2 tablespoons milk, heated
2/3 cup sifted confectioners' sugar
1 1/2 cups finely flaked unsweetened coconut

Filling
3 egg yolks
1 1/4 cups milk
1/4 cup sugar
1 envelope unflavored gelatin
1 1/2 cups heavy whipping cream
1/4 cup confectioners' sugar
1/4 teaspoon salt
2 teaspoons vanilla extract

Parfaits
1/4 cup flaked unsweetened coconut, lightly toasted
1/4 cup toasted slivered almonds, finely chopped
1/2 (1-ounce) square unsweetened chocolate, grated

For the crust, grease a baking sheet. Combine the chocolate and butter in a nonstick saucepan over low heat and stir until melted. Combine the hot milk and confectioners' sugar in a small bowl and stir into the chocolate mixture. Stir in the coconut. Press into a thin 8-inch square on the prepared cookie sheet. Chill until cold. Cut into sixteen 2-inch squares.

For the filling, beat the egg yolks in the top of a double boiler over simmering water until frothy. Whisk in the milk slowly. Add the sugar and stir until dissolved. Sprinkle the gelatin over the top of the egg mixture and stir until dissolved. Cook for 5 minutes or until the custard coats the back of a spoon, stirring constantly. Chill until the mixture thickens, stirring occasionally. Beat until smooth. Whip the cream in a mixing bowl until soft peaks form. Add the sugar, salt and vanilla gradually, beating until stiff peaks form. Fold the whipped cream gently into the custard mixture. If the custard has cooled too long and hardened before adding the whipped cream, heat the custard slightly, and then beat it vigorously to reach custard consistency.

For the parfaits, crumble 1 square of crust into each of 8 parfait or wine glasses. Top each with 1/4 cup plus 1 tablespoon of the cream filling. Repeat the layers. Chill until serving time. Top each parfait with the coconut, almonds and grated chocolate.

Brandy Baked Pears with Sherry Cream Sauce

Yield: 10 to 12 servings

This is the best thing that ever happened to pears. Serve this luscious dessert in Champagne glasses to impress your guests. They'll want to scoop up every last drop of the irresistible sauce.

Baked Pears
3 (14-ounce) cans pear halves, drained
1 cup chopped walnuts
1/4 cup (1/2 stick) butter
1 cup sugar
3/4 cup brandy

Sherry Cream Sauce
2 tablespoons cornstarch
1/4 cup sugar
1 cup cream sherry
2 cups cream
1 tablespoon vanilla extract

For the pears, preheat the oven to 350 degrees. Arrange the pears in a 9×13-inch baking dish cut side up. Fill the cavities with the walnuts. Combine the butter, sugar and brandy in a saucepan. Bring to a boil. Cook until the sugar dissolves, stirring constantly. Simmer for 10 minutes. Pour over the pears. You may prepare to this point and chill, covered, for 8 hours, if desired. Bake for 15 minutes or until the sauce begins to bubble.

For the cream sauce, combine the cornstarch and sugar in a saucepan. Add the sherry and cream and stir until the cornstarch is dissolved. Cook over medium heat until the sauce thickens and bubbles, stirring constantly. Let stand until slightly cool. Stir in the vanilla. Chill until serving time.

To serve, place 1 large warm pear half or 2 small halves and some of the brandy syrup in each serving dish. Top with the chilled Sherry Cream Sauce.

A Gift to Share

The scenic views of Allied Arts Guild depicted on the cover and in the chapter openers of this book are from original watercolors and oil paintings by Carolyn Hofstetter, one of our own longtime members.

The original paintings of the beautiful gardens and historic architecture, captured through the eyes of a talented artist, were presented as very special gifts to members with 30 years' service or outstanding achievement. Over the years, many of our members qualified for this award and received the coveted watercolors at the yearly Membership Teas.

All of the recipients graciously allowed us into their homes so that we could professionally photograph their paintings for this book. What an honor to not only have received one of these beautiful works of art, but also to have it displayed in this cookbook.

Thank you to all the 30-year veterans and outstanding achievers who worked so hard to earn these highly valued gifts and for sharing them with us in this cookbook.

Lemon Crisp

Yield: 8 servings

This old-time Restaurant favorite still remains in style with veteran volunteers and guests alike.

Crust
1/2 cup (1 stick) butter, softened
2/3 cup packed brown sugar
1 cup all-purpose flour
1/2 teaspoon baking soda
1/2 cup finely chopped flaked coconut
3/4 cup finely crushed butter crackers

Lemon Custard
1 1/4 cups sugar
3 tablespoons cornstarch
3 tablespoons all-purpose flour
1 1/2 cups water
3 egg yolks, beaten
2 tablespoons butter
1 1/2 teaspoons grated lemon zest
1/3 cup fresh lemon juice

For the crust, grease a 9×9-inch baking pan. Preheat the oven to 350 degrees. Cream the butter and brown sugar in a mixing bowl until light and fluffy. Add the flour, baking soda, coconut and cracker crumbs and mix well. Press 2 cups of the crumb mixture evenly in the prepared baking pan, reserving the remaining crumb mixture. Bake for 10 minutes.

For the custard, maintain the oven temperature at 350 degrees. Combine the sugar, cornstarch and flour in a medium saucepan. Add the water gradually, stirring constantly. Cook over medium-high heat until the mixture boils and thickens, stirring constantly. Remove from the heat. Stir a small amount of the hot mixture into the beaten egg yolks; stir the egg yolks into the hot mixture. Cook for 1 minute, stirring constantly. Remove from the heat. Stir in the butter, lemon zest and lemon juice. Pour the custard over the baked crust. Sprinkle evenly with the reserved crumb mixture. Bake on the top rack of the oven for 20 minutes. Serve with whipped cream.

Rhubarb Apple Crunch

Yield: 6 to 8 servings

The juices of these two fruits combine to give this dessert a sweet, tangy taste. Served with vanilla ice cream, it's marvelous!

2 cups (1-inch chunks) rhubarb
1 cup sliced peeled sweet apples, such as Cortland,
   Jonathan, Red Spy, Spartan, Golden Delicious,
   P ippin or Gravenstein
1 cup granulated sugar
3 tablespoons all-purpose flour
1/2 teaspoon cinnamon
11/2 cups quick-cooking rolled oats
1 cup packed light brown sugar
1 cup all-purpose flour
1/2 cup (1 stick) butter, cut into 1-inch pieces

Butter a 9×9-inch baking pan. Preheat the oven to 375 degrees. Combine the rhubarb, apples, granulated sugar, 3 tablespoons flour and cinnamon in a bowl and mix well. Spread evenly in the prepared baking pan. Combine the oats, brown sugar, 1 cup flour and the butter in a bowl and mix until crumbly. Sprinkle evenly over the fruit mixture. Bake for 40 minutes or until lightly browned. Serve warm topped with vanilla ice cream or whipped cream.

The Brass Candleholders

In the early 1960s, Auxiliary members were searching for new candleholders to adorn the Restaurant tables. They absolutely loved a metal holder that one member had bought in Japan the previous year. When no other candleholder would suffice, they sent the next member who would be traveling to Japan on a mission. Her job was to purchase thirty of the same attractive metal holders, which were painted black and were just perfect for our needs. The thrifty traveler ordered three dozen at $3.00 apiece and shipped them to many different members in order to save money on customs fees.

A few years later, another member decided the holders needed a thorough cleaning to rid them of accumulated candle wax. To her horror she also removed the black paint! The metal underneath, however, turned out to be a lovely bronze color, which was even more attractive than the paint.

Forty years later these lovely candleholders were still adorning the tables.

Frozen Strawberry Delight

Yield: 12 servings

A succulent strawberry filling is sandwiched between a crunchy and buttery crumb crust for a dessert that is better than ice cream. Serve this treat on a warm summer day. Freeze it for at least six hours before serving.

1 cup all-purpose flour
1/4 cup packed brown sugar
1/2 cup (1 stick) butter, melted
1/2 cup chopped walnuts
2 egg whites
1 cup granulated sugar
1 (10-ounce) package frozen sweetened strawberries, thawed
2 tablespoons lemon juice
1 cup heavy whipping cream, whipped,
  or 4 ounces whipped topping

Butter a 9×13-inch baking pan and set aside. Preheat the oven to 350 degrees. Combine the flour, brown sugar, butter and walnuts in a bowl and mix well. Spread in an ungreased shallow baking pan. Bake for 20 minutes or until browned, stirring occasionally. Let stand until cool and then break up into crumbs. Combine the egg whites, granulated sugar, undrained strawberries and lemon juice in a large mixing bowl and beat until stiff peaks form. Whip the cream in another bowl until stiff peaks form. Fold into the strawberry mixture. Sprinkle 1/2 of the crumb mixture in the bottom of the buttered baking pan. Spread the strawberry filling evenly over the crumbs and top with the remaining crumbs. Freeze, tightly covered with foil, for at least 6 hours or up to 8 hours. Cut into squares and top each serving with a dollop of whipped cream and/or sliced fresh strawberries.

Leaving the Restaurant

" …It didn't seem hard.
We were young, and we felt
we were doing a service for
sick children, and we loved it."

Mrs. William (Marge) Pabst
Palo Alto Auxiliary President, 1939

Contributors

The Core Cookbook Team

Luisa Pliska, Co-Leader   Donna Jones, Co-Leader
Gail Sachs, Secretary   Wanda Hart, Consulting
Mary Hicks, Recipes   Lenore Lafayette, Research

Tastes, Tales and Traditions came to life as a result of the Core Cookbook Team's dedication and perseverance. This diverse group of six women developed the theme, produced the business plan, established the process, and managed each step of the project from conception to final editing. Through all the ups and downs, the team members never lost sight of their vision and vigorously pursued their challenging goals every step of the way. What has evolved, in addition to a seventy-year legacy, is a lasting friendship among six independent and talented members of the Palo Alto Auxiliary. It was truly a labor of love.

Non-Recipe Text

Marty Johnson, a longtime member of the Palo Alto Auxiliary and Editor of the organization's Newsletter, drafted the special event stories and the majority of sidebars for this cookbook. With a B.A. in English Literature, a Master's in Education, and a knack for good writing, Marty stood out as the perfect candidate to translate into words the rich history of the Auxiliary. Her charming and lively style of writing comes not only from a great education, but also from a full and active life. A happily married mother of two boys, Marty dedicates her life to volunteer work and spends her spare time reading, cooking, quilting, and caring for orphaned robins.

History

Sally (Sarah) Bush, a veteran of the Palo Alto Auxiliary since 1967, and Historian since 1980, supplied the history used in the writing of this cookbook. Sally has served on several committees, including menu planning, but found her niche documenting the oral and written history of the Organization. This pleasant stint also gave Sally exposure to many recipes, as well as knowledge of our loyal customers' taste for food.

Original Watercolors and Oils

Carolyn Hofstetter, a member of the Palo Alto Auxiliary for more than four decades and an award-winning artist, painted the oils and watercolors depicted on the cover and in the chapter openers of this cookbook. Carolyn majored in art at Stanford University and taught oil painting in her studio and on location for thirty years. Her work has been shown in Europe and can be seen in several Bay Area galleries. She has more than 1,000 paintings in public and private collections. Carolyn considers herself primarily a landscape painter and says, "In oil or watercolor, my artwork reflects what I see in the beauty of life around me." And so it is, with her beautiful paintings of the Allied Arts Guild settings featured in this cookbook.

Index

Tastes, Tales and Traditions

Palo Alto Auxiliary for Children, Inc.
75 Arbor Road, Suite C • Menlo Park, California 94025
Telephone: (650) 324-2588 • Fax: (650) 324-2552
Email: aagr2@sbcglobal.net

Sold To: *(Please print.)*

Name _____

Address _____

City _____ State _____ Zip _____

Ship To: *(Attach list if additional shipping addresses.)*

Name _____

Address _____

City _____ State _____ Zip _____

Quantity	Your Order		Total
_____	*Tastes, Tales and Traditions* at $27.70 per book	$	_____
_____	California residents add 8.25% sales tax*	$	_____
_____	Shipping and handling at $5.00 per book	$	_____
	Total	$	_____

*If shipping outside California, omit tax.

Method of Payment: [ ] MasterCard   [ ] VISA   [ ] Check enclosed payable to the Palo Alto Auxiliary

Name (as appears on card) _____

Card Number _____ Expiration Date _____

Signature _____

Telephone _____ Fax _____ Email _____

Sign Up To Be A Volunteer

*If you would like to serve your community in a most enjoyable and rewarding way,
the Palo Alto Auxiliary is your answer. Whatever your skill level, we have a job for you.
To inquire about becoming a volunteer, call, fax, or email us (see above).*

Photocopies of this form will be accepted.